THE
BITCOIN
MINER'S
ALMANAC

THE
BITCOIN
MINER'S
ALMANAC

Where Code Meets Business and Everything in Between

ROBERT WARREN

BITCOIN MAGAZINE
≋⫼ BOOKS™
Bitcoin Magazine Books
Nashville, TN

The Bitcoin Miners Almanac by Robert Warren

ISBN 979-8-9891326-3-8 (Paperback)

ISBN 979-8-9891326-4-5 (eBook)

BITCOIN MAGAZINE
≋|||ʼ BOOKS™

Published by Bitcoin Magazine Books
An imprint of BTC Media, LLC
300 10th Avenue South, Nashville, TN 37203

Address all queries to contact@btcmedia.org

Interior design by MediaNeighbours.com

Graphics Illustrated by José Bam

As to methods there may be a million and then some, but principles are few. The man who grasps principles can successfully select his own methods. The man who tries methods, ignoring principles, is sure to have trouble.

—Harrington Emerson
[Not Ralph Waldo Emerson]

CONTENTS

INTRODUCTION

Forget about Bitcoin. Abandon discussions around BIPs, Core development, forks, and key management. Instead, think about a shoebox. Make it out of metal and make it heavy. Got it? Now plug that shoebox into an electrical outlet and an internet connection. It will whine incessantly like cicadas on a hot summer night while spitting out a perpetual blast of hot, hot air. As a professional shoebox operator, your job is to make your machine run profitably. Forever, if possible. This, in essence, is Bitcoin mining. We purchase these alien machines, set up facilities, and work towards mastering the nascent art of taming cyber hornets.

Why would any sane human participate in this activity? What could possibly compel thousands, if not tens of thousands of individuals, to join the madness of plugging in metal shoeboxes and producing immense amounts of heat and noise? It sounds batty to the casual observer, yet this is the heart of Bitcoin mining. Distributed across the world, in locations as varied as personal homes and businesses, greenhouses, solar and wind farms, power plants, large and small substations on a grid near you, community dumps, and even oil and gas well sites, individuals are developing the technologies and business strategies that allow them to operate maniacal shoeboxes in every corner of the world.

In the new world of professional shoebox operators, entire divisions have spun off to address the various scales and environmental conditions shoebox operators work in. For the small-scale shoebox operator, an entire market segment of home shoebox operation has emerged, with special computer boards, fans, and ducting that allow for safe and quiet shoebox operation without driving your children or spouse insane from the heat and noise. Mid-sized professional shoebox operators negotiate with small electrical producers and organizations with excess power in the hope of signing deals that allow them to deploy their special shoebox racks and container systems at appealing power rates. They often utilize a suite of industrial-looking containerized solutions (larger, shipping container-sized metal shoeboxes that fit hundreds of these smaller shoeboxes within them), industrial power strips, and even large industrial fans and filters to keep the shoeboxes happily screaming away.

The largest shoebox operators trade publicly in markets you know by name and hear about on the daily news. They buy massive tracts of land near large-scale electrical producers or grid-scale switches and erect warehouse-style buildings of custom-engineered design that run 100s of feet in length, fitting tens of thousands of machines from wall to wall.

This world of professional shoebox operation even has a high-tech sector, where programmers, engineers, and builders experiment with dunking the shoeboxes in cooling oils, by running cool water loops through their specialized bodies, or by developing early-stage hardware, software, or firmware that allows these devices to run faster, slower, cooler, hotter, or under various other performance conditions.

All of this effort is for the singular purpose of gaining an edge by operating shoeboxes profitably.

You would think that with all this effort being poured into shoebox operation, we would have reached an optimal state. But in the world of professional shoebox operation, the opposite is true. We are only at the event horizon of innovation. A vast world of possibilities stretches before us. Everywhere you turn, someone is emerging from the woodwork with a technological or business solution to run shoeboxes more optimally in more and more variable conditions. In fact, in only the last three years, the amount of shoebox-related work being done (measured in something called Exahash) has nearly quadrupled.[1]

Shoebox operation is no small game.

In the world of Bitcoin, the shoebox operators—the Bitcoin miners—are seen as the most ephemeral of characters. They speak in joules per terahash, megawatts, and phases. They talk of pools, FPPS, PPLNS, firmware upgrades, cooling loops, and even HVAC and plumbing. An early-stage Bitcoiner, having spent their days poring over every podcast to be found and buying stacks of books from their local retailer to understand the game theoretic mechanics of the Bitcoin network, will struggle to understand what these electrically powered maniacs are talking about. Bitcoin mining is *supposed* to be the method by which the blockchain organizes itself and issues new Bitcoin. What on earth does that have to do with substations or HVAC?

To the wider outside world, Bitcoin miners are a rare niche, a seemingly heterogeneous assembly of mad scientists speaking a foreign language. Like the machines themselves, they are a spree of hornets chaotically racing through the air with no apparent center or direction. And yet, to Bitcoin miners themselves, the center is obvious and the incentives are clear.

What unifies and compels Bitcoin miners, regardless of scale, type, or style, is simple economic profit, gotten by playing a simple digital game that everyone knows the rules to. What does running a shoebox have to do with Bitcoin? Sometimes, nothing at all. This cacophony of Bitcoin mining businesses has interests as varied as waste management, the incentivization of renewable energy sources, heating, personal privacy, and occasionally even the acquisition of Bitcoin itself.

There is no immediate need to understand why a Bitcoin mining machine does what it does to understand what motivates Bitcoin miners. The question is better resolved by first interrogating *what* a Bitcoin mining machine does, then working out from the shoebox into the world of *how*—apprehending the *why* through the voices of the operators themselves. Only then are we equipped to finally point our eyes to the skies to better envision where we might be headed.

This book is fundamentally an exploration of the game of Bitcoin mining and the many ways it has emerged and continues to evolve in the world around us. The goal is to make a seemingly complex muddle simple and lift the veil on the profusion of electrical, HVAC, and computer jargon for the curious masses, whether they are self-described Bitcoiners or not.

We'll explore this game in two parts. Part One is called *The World Through A Shoebox: A Cyber Hornet Anatomy Lesson*. Part Two is called *The Business of Bitcoin Mining: For Every Miner There's a Model*. We'll then wrap things up with a brief conclusion.

Part One
The World Through a Shoebox:
A Cyber Hornet Anatomy Lesson

We begin by investigating the Application Specific Integrated Circuit (ASIC) miner, a malapropism that is the ire of professional chip builders everywhere (ASIC refers to a chip, not an entire machine). Briefly tracking the emergence of the Bitcoin ASIC, we will introduce the four necessary components of the machine: the power supply, the control board, the hashboard, and the cooling mechanism. With the machine explained, we'll introduce the three physical connections required by all mining machines: an internet connection, an electrical cord, and a method for regulating temperature.

We will then do a deep dive into the internet connection and the game Bitcoin miners play within the Bitcoin network. The internet connection opens up the world of machine software, firmware, and pool rewards (while this exploration touches on the world of shadowy super coders, along with things like hard forks and BIP proposals, enthusiasts of deep technical discussions will be disappointed.) We learn that these machines exist for a single goal: to hash. A first (but not the only incentive) emerges: Bitcoin mining machines are run to generate revenue.

We then explore the electricity that runs the shoebox and how professional shoebox operators acquire and manage it. Electricity is not equally accessible across the world nor equally created by various forms of generation. We will introduce and explain the most common mechanism Bitcoin miners use to power their machines—the grid. However, there is a growing community of operators who specifically stay off-grid. Exploring their world leads us to move one additional step up the supply chain to commodities and various raw sources of energy that are converted into electricity. This exploration helps us understand the many ways energy is used inefficiently or wasted entirely prior to ever being delivered to a socket near you.

From the internet and electricity, we expand our discussion to the final physical necessity of machine operation: cooling.

Whether you use air-cooled machines with their screaming fans, immersion machines requiring gallons of dielectric oil, or hydro machines needing custom racking and precisely monitored water compositions depends heavily on your strategic goals and philosophy as a business. While hydro and immersion mining dissipate heat more efficiently than air-cooled miners, they are not always the "best" decision for miners. Limitations around operational location, hazards, and (most importantly) cost should inform which method of cooling a miner chooses independent of machine efficiency and total terahash.

Then there are the numerous ways a miner can choose to run these machines to generate revenue. Here a Doctor Suess-esque symphony of questions arise:

Can I run it in a house?
Can I run it for my spouse?
Shall I hash upon the moon?
Must ASICs always sing their tune?

Setting up facilities and keeping machines operating happily is both an art and a science, requiring adhering to the principles of machine protection and temperature regulation and a diverse set of skills that align more with plumbing, electrical, and general contracting work than the prototypical "high tech" of the current Bitcoin space. As we delve into cooling mechanisms, we naturally explore the various setups and techniques operators use to keep their ASICs screaming.

Mining operators come in all shapes and sizes. Managing a single machine in your basement is worlds apart in technical and operational complexity from a mid-sized warehouse or mega-mining deployment with tens of thousands of computers, leading to a discussion of farm footprint and scale. Delving into the common methods of housing machines from environmental damage and managing temperature efficiently allows us to discuss the pros, cons, and limiting factors of various deployment styles.

We end Part One with an overview of the basics of Bitcoin mining as a business. Like any business, miners must generate more revenue than expenses. They generate revenue by selling the value of the hashes they produce over time and by finding and capitalizing on asymmetries in related industries. On the other side of the profit equation, miners control their expenses by managing them, with machines their largest capital expense and electricity their largest operational expense.

Part Two
The Business of Bitcoin Mining:
For Every Miner There's a Model

What compels operators to invest immense sums of capital into establishing facilities of various sizes and types and operating these machines at scale? It can't *truly* be to generate some magical internet money we seem to only hear about every four years after it has emerged again from the doorstep of financial death and destruction. In Part Two we examine real-world examples of the seemingly disparate strategies and techniques Bitcoin miners use to form the basis of a profitable business.

Through a series of structured interviews that share the voices of actual Bitcoin mine operators, we begin to appreciate that mining machines can do more than simply generate hashes. The what, when, how, and where of energy and the subsequent electrons that energy can produce create secondary incentives for Bitcoin miners entirely unrelated to the pure profit motive of generating revenues in Bitcoin. The great divergence in type, size, and location in Bitcoin mining operations is explained through the voices of operators, and their various business models take shape as we discover why they are able to generate a profit not only in massive facilities on the US grid but by using remote hydroelectric dams in Africa or oil and gas wells in Oklahoma.

For example, shoebox operators can support themselves by producing revenues in Bitcoin and by playing a strategic game with the energy and electricity used to run their operation. But as we discover below, miners can add an additional incentive to the system by making heat generation—that nuisance output of these screaming machines—a source of revenue. By lining up the output heat of a Bitcoin miner with the input heat required for other applications, like your home water heater and HVAC system, the limitations and costs of heat generation are vastly reduced, and a second business model takes shape.

Stories such as these only begin to scratch the surface and potential of the industry. As the subtitle of Part Two says, for every miner there is a model. Our interviews span everyone in the industry, from an early computing tech engineer and a Bitcoin privacy advocate to a public corporate CEO. Despite different sizes and types of mining operations, each has found a profitable and worthwhile business model using Bitcoin mining as the backbone.

Conclusion

We close out the text with a brief discussion of the future. We are early in mining innovation, systems, and technologies, in a word, everything oriented around method and optimization. It is easy to make vast predictions about the Earth-shattering consequences of our fledgling monetary system; in fact, you gain immense popularity and clout through an unrelenting perma-bull attitude. But it is more difficult—but also more worthwhile—to move slowly, study deeply, and emerge out the other side *just as optimistic* as the many flag wavers and clout chasers, but armed with knowledge of the hardware behind Bitcoin mining and an understanding of the business models that are possible armed with that knowledge.

PART ONE
THE WORLD THROUGH A SHOEBOX:
A CYBER HORNET ANATOMY LESSON

W**hy begin our** exploration with the mining machine itself and not the theory or role of Bitcoin mining in network function? In short, because everyone secretly hates theory and the Bitcoin mining industry as we know it is barely ten years old. The youthfulness of this space means there are no seasoned masters of the universe of Bitcoin mining and no pedigreed operators from impressive institutions well-versed in the theoretical and practical norms of our space. And while I'm not an historian of early American innovations, I can assure you that while the Model T was gaining in popularity throughout the early 20th Century, nobody, except the most insufferable attendees of Gatsby's parties wanted to talk about supply chain management, innovation on the newfangled assembly line, or the strategic Michigan locations of Ford factories.[2] People wanted a cheap way to get around. It was far more sanitary and convenient to have a car next to your house than a barn full of hay and a stable full of horses. You don't need theory to explain to you why it's better—you want the wind in your hair and the open road in front of you.

While Bitcoin mining may hardly excite the average individual in the way a ripping 42 mph down a country road in an early Model T can, the immediate effects of Bitcoin mining are reverberating across multiple industries with the same technical significance. Already a diverse set of industry operators, from oil and gas behemoths to aquaponic farms, are discovering the compelling uses of these machines. To fully understand those uses, it's necessary for us to have a preliminary understanding of the parts of the machine—the "What."

In the same way a first-time driver would require introductory training to understand the parts and functions of their brand-new vehicle, a Bitcoin miner should grasp the parts of their machine that make it go. Fortunately, there are only four parts to every Bitcoin mining machine: a power supply, a control board, a hashboard, and a cooling system. By better understanding these four pieces, we can begin to understand the world that feeds the machine and the businesses and strategies that emerge.

The Four Parts of a Bitcoin Miner

When I was a sophomore in high school enrolled in a darkroom photography course, I distinctly remember the teacher standing at the front of the class and confidently declaring that every camera had five parts. A lens, an aperture, a shutter, a light-tight box, and a recording medium. This thought baffled me. Looking at images of historical 6x6 view cameras, twin lens reflex cameras, our family Polaroid camera, and soon my very first digital camera—a Nikon D50 with a whopping 6.1 megapixels of resolution[3]—I couldn't readily disprove his statement. While the form of a camera has changed, film became a digital sensor, apertures

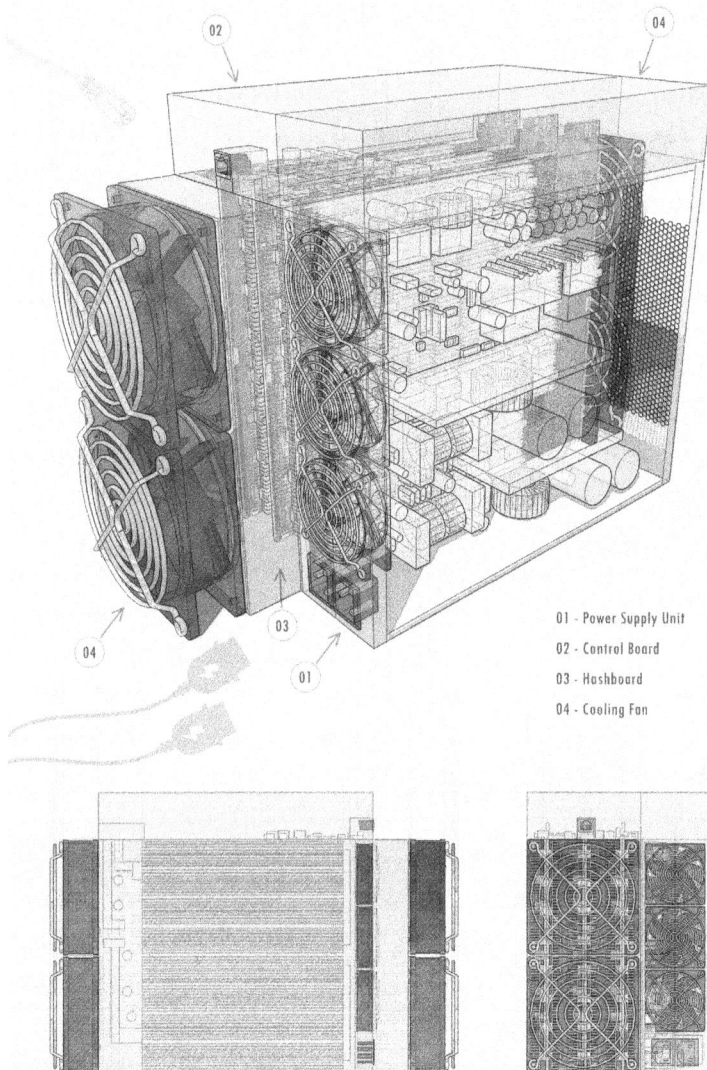

01 - Power Supply Unit
02 - Control Board
03 - Hashboard
04 - Cooling Fan

Figure 1: *An illustration of a Bitmain style mining machine with the four component parts labeled.*

changed size and shape, and shutters radically changed form and speed, every camera I found contained the same five simple parts.

Years later I would sit in a booth in Envie Espresso Bar and Cafe on Decatur St. in New Orleans and click "Buy" on a Nikon D800 with a whopping 36.3 megapixels of resolution[4]—an unfathomably powerful camera to my high school self—but a camera nonetheless, consisting of the exact same five parts.

Innovation in Bitcoin mining machines follows this technological trend. While the various elements of the machine change, refine, and develop for specific applications and purposes, they will all comprise four general parts, a power source, a control board, a hashboard, and a cooling mechanism, and they will all incrementally improve over time.

In the earliest days of Bitcoin, mining was performed on household computers using CPUs (central processing units), then quickly advanced to GPUs (general processing units), briefly dabbled in an alien technology called the FPGA (Field Programmable Gate Array), before the launch of the first dedicated Bitcoin mining ASIC by Avalon in 2013, which has set the operational platform since.[5] We won't explore these early versions of Bitcoin mining hardware. We will focus instead on the current footprint of Bitcoin mining machines, which has not drastically changed since the creation of that first Bitcoin ASIC, because at this point the industry appears to be driving towards optimization and not radical reformulation.

The Power Supply

The lifeblood of Bitcoin mining is electricity, specifically direct current (DC). This is distinct from alternating current (AC), which is how electricity is transmitted and delivered to residences,

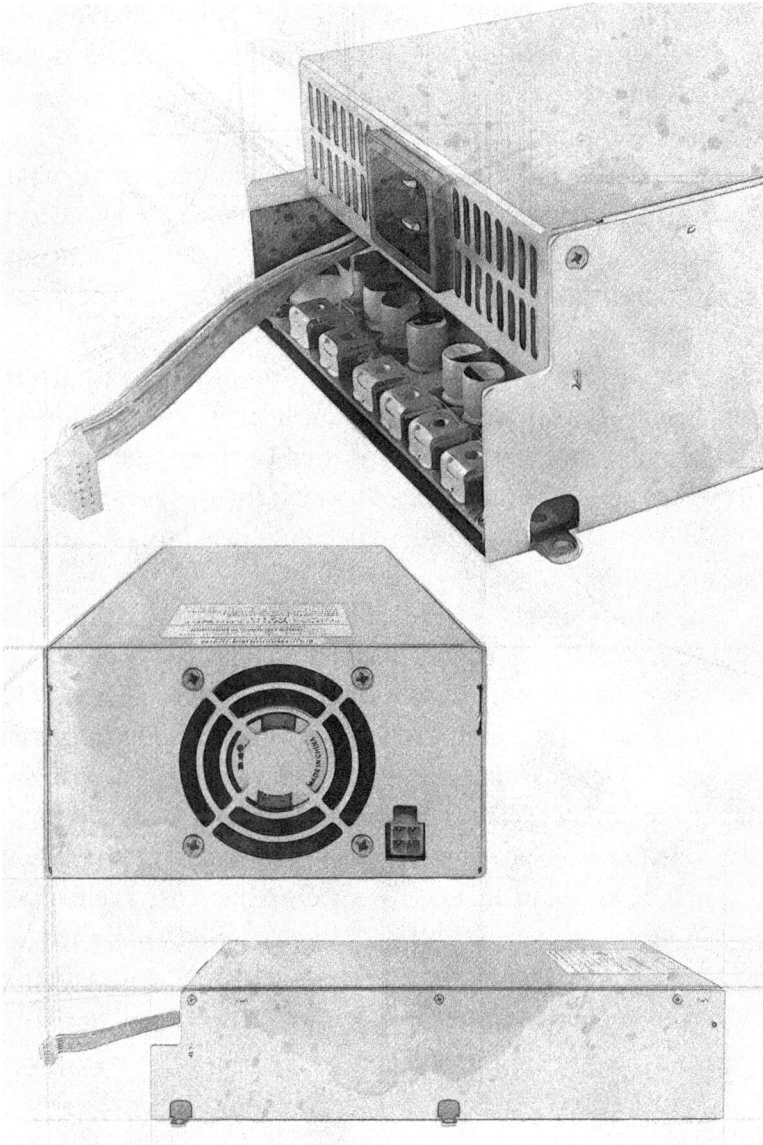

Figure 2: *A power supply unit, or PSU, which delivers direct current power to the hash board from a source of alternating current.*

commercial, and industrial spaces all over the world. We'll discuss electrical generation and transmission in greater detail when exploring Bitcoin miner operation, but for our immediate purposes, it's enough to understand that the power supply of a mining machine is a unit, typically detachable and swappable, that converts incoming AC power into consumable DC power for the ASIC chips to operate. However, inverting the incoming AC power to DC does not come without a cost. There are efficiency losses associated with this necessary conversion, often from 5%-20% of total energy input.[6] Some ingenious tinkers have discovered a way around this efficiency loss by running DC current from a source of generation (typically solar arrays) directly to the chips, forgoing the need for the power supply unit entirely. However, these implementations are not broadly commercialized today.[7]

The power supply is a critically important component. It is what connects the individual machine to a source of incoming electricity. In this role, it is tasked with keeping a continuous and steady supply of DC power to the machine while enduring variations in daily or seasonal temperature and often harsh environmental conditions. When a machine fails to run, excessive heat often overheats the power supply unit past its ability to cool itself and power the rest of the machine safely. Much like scrolling X/Twitter on your iPhone in a sauna, a Bitcoin miner will stop working when ambient temperatures become too punishing. In the case of air-cooled machines, this is often between 95F to 104F.[8]

The Control Board

The Bitcoin miner needs a brain, and the control board is specifically designed to fulfill that purpose. A preliminary Google search

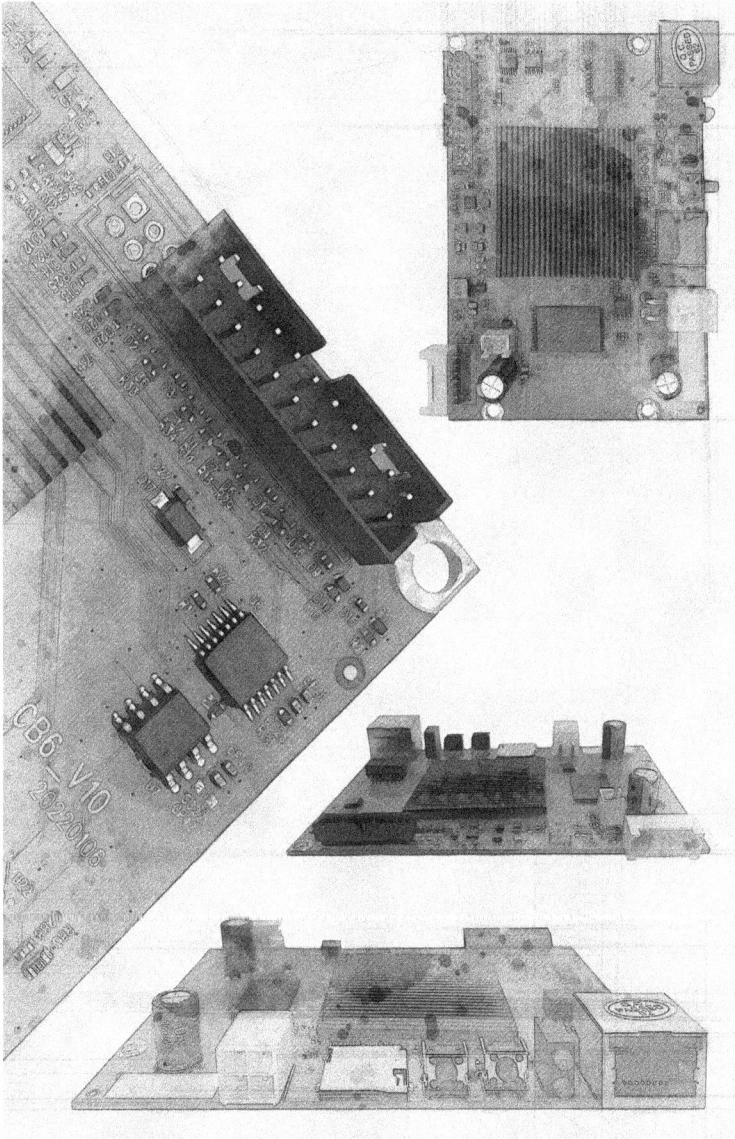

Figure 3: *An illustration of a control board, the brain of the Bitcoin mining machine.*

for "Bitcoin Miner Control Board" will send you down a rabbit hole of technical discussions around Beagle Bones, Zynqs, and AMLogics.9 But for the sake of making it through this book in one piece, you should ignore that as quickly as possible and focus on the most important aspect of the control board—it is the brain and the connectivity of the entire Bitcoin miner. The control board is what tells the machine how and when to operate and directs performance across various programmed or environmental conditions. It is also how the machine connects to the internet via a common ethernet cable—one of the only three physical connections required for machine operation.

The control board is where device firmware lives, which can be thought of as the operating system of the machine.[10] This firmware can be the stock firmware that comes from the device manufacturer, or it can be an aftermarket offering, designed to allow the machine to operate under special conditions or controls.

The most important thing to remember is that the control board is the *brain* of the Bitcoin miner. It tells everyone else what to do, and relays what it is doing and has done to the rest of the world via an internet connection. There are some models of mining machines that put parts of the brain on the hashboard or in the power supply, but they all function in the same way—as a brain for the machine.

The Hashboard

If our discussion of the four parts of the Bitcoin miner were an MTV Cribs Tour, the hashboard is undoubtedly where the magic happens. It is the location of the most fervent technical innovation and the most heated discussions around machine operation.

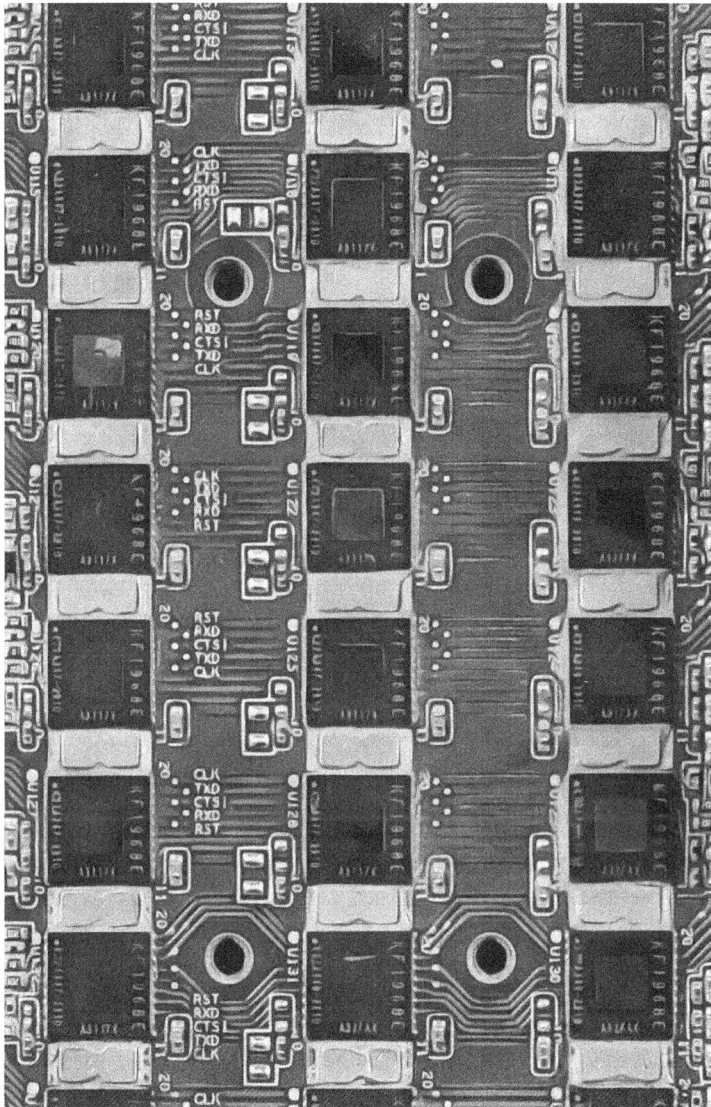

Figure 4: *A close up of a bitcoin miner hash board with compo-nent ASIC chips.*

The hashboard, or chipset, is the aggregation of individual ASIC chips, often from as few as 70 to over 300 individual chips on a single electrified board.[11] Each of these chips performs a single function, known as hashing, trillions upon trillions of times over the course of its functional life. When you add up all of those chips onto a single hashboard, then put those hashboards into a machine, you have a single device that generates trillions of hashes every second, commonly expressed in terahash (T).

Over the years the total terahash a single machine produces has grown by leaps and bounds. For example, one large manufacturer, Bitmain, released an ASIC in 2013 called the S1 that produced .18T, an incredibly large number at the time.[12] Ten years later, Bitmain delivers a machine called the S19XP that generates 141T.[13] This is a 783-fold improvement in terahash against the original S1, the equivalent of going from horse and buggy (one literal horsepower) to a Bugatti in ten short years. With this in mind, you might be inclined to believe the industry only builds machines with the largest total terahash in mind, but you would be only half right.

Hashboards are not only built to produce the greatest amount of work per second but are also designed to consume DC power from the power supply unit in the *most efficient way possible.* There are hundreds if not thousands of hashboard configurations, oriented in slightly different ways for various technical and operational reasons. The technology behind these design and build choices is incredible and far beyond our current scope. However, there is one key principle we should understand when it comes to the hashboard and the ASIC chips that live and work on it—the goal of the game is efficiency, and efficiency moves from the chip outwards.

You can think of Bitcoin miner efficiency in the same way you think about vehicle efficiency. If your car made you money for every mile you traveled, but how much you made depending on how much gas you consumed, you better believe you would be selling the Toyota Tundra and buying a Prius the next morning. In the same vein, the ASIC chip performs work in the way a car engine moves a vehicle, but instead of consuming gasoline to travel a particular distance, the ASIC consumes electricity and produces work in the form of hashes for the Bitcoin network.

Instead of measuring efficiency in miles per gallon, as we do with motor vehicles, we use the concept of joules per terahash (J/T), where joules are the amount of energy you put in, and terahash is the amount of work you get out. Unlike motor vehicles, where you might aim for a higher number of miles per gallon to represent greater vehicle efficiency, we are instead looking for the *smallest* number of joules required to produce 1 terahash of work. This is the goal of peak efficiency, and the Bitcoin mining industry strives to build machines that can generate the highest amount of total work (T) with the smallest amount of total energy used (J/T).

The Cooling

The hashboard gets the glory in the world of Bitcoin mining, but the cooling mechanism of the machine is the strong, silent hero. Why is this the case? A Bitcoin mining machine consumes electricity and performs work using the ASIC chips assembled across the hashboard. As that work is completed, the electricity used to perform that work has to go *somewhere*. It is at this point every middle and high school science teacher reading this book is salivating, waiting for me to deliver the next sentence:

Energy cannot be created or destroyed.[14]

(Feel free to breathe a sigh of relief now.)

We bring up the law of energy conservation because for every watt of electricity a Bitcoin mining machine consumes, it must shed that energy in the form of heat. If you have ever brought your iPhone into the sauna with you, you are familiar with the need for electronics to shed heat as you watched your cell phone self-protectively brick itself until you were done having a *schvitz*.

Like all electronics, Bitcoin mining machines must be cooled, and there are currently three ways to do it: air, oil immersion, or hydro cooling. Cooling efficiency changes drastically from air to

Figure 5: *Machine cooling fans—one method of heat removal from mining machines.*

immersion to hydro and can be measured with a single convenient metric from mechanical engineering called the heat transfer coefficient. It is a well-studied and conveniently calculable metric that, for our purposes, illustrates the hierarchy of cooling efficiency with the power of fancy engineering.

Air cooling is by far the cheapest and most convenient method of cooling a Bitcoin miner and can be found almost anywhere Bitcoin mining happens. The perpetual whine of the high-volume fans that cool the miners has become so recognizable that Microstrategy CEO Michael Saylor characterized the industry as "a swarm of cyber hornets," apropos both the machines and culture of the people in the space.[15] While air cooling is the quickest and most cost-effective way to cool a miner, it is the least efficient cooling method. You have to move a substantial volume of air to effectively cool your mining operation and are often at the mercy of local weather conditions or seasonal variations.

Immersion cooling is a heat removal strategy by which machines are dunked into tanks of circulating non-reactive oils instead of using fans to dissipate heat. As the machine runs and generates heat, the oil is circulated over the surfaces of the machine and is either run directly to a dry cooler to be cooled (imagine a big version of your car radiator) or through a plate exchanger (imagine a metal sandwich that lets one liquid cool another liquid without them mixing) and then to a dry cooler. The differences between these two systems are what is called a single-loop or double-loop setup. We won't go into deep detail regarding these two options, but suffice it to say there are good reasons for each.

Upon introducing immersion cooling, you may be asking yourself, "Hmm. That seems like a lot of extra equipment. That sounds expensive." You would be spot on. Immersion cooling requires specialty tanks, specialty fluids, and additional pumps, coolers, and infrastructure to function. All of this is in addition to the steps required to purchase specialty immersion machines or modify machines originally built for air cooling and adapt them for immersion in oil.

This may appear an unreasonable effort and expense, but the reason operators go through the trouble of immersion is because machine operation becomes far more stable through changing external conditions and cooling efficiency improves dramatically. As the seasons and weather change around your Bitcoin mine, an immersion setup is far more likely to not suffer daily or seasonal overheating where an air-cooled system may struggle.

The current "final boss" of mining machine cooling is the hydro-miner. These are nascent offerings in the market, but are likely to continue to expand rapidly as they exceed the cooling efficiency of immersion mining—and in key ways reduce the complexity of the overall system. A hydro mining rig, instead of being immersed in a cooling oil, is specifically designed to run a special preparation of water through the machine itself. (Don't worry, the water never touches any of the electrical components—it's segregated into a cooling block or piping.) These Bitcoin mining machines resemble the state-of-the-art in commercial datacenter cooling that use similar technology and footprints.

The specially prepared water solution runs through the body of the machine itself, entering cool and emerging hot, then travels through an external dry cooler to be cooled down, then back to the input to repeat the cycle again. This is the same way a single-loop immersion setup might operate but with a water solution instead of immersion oil. Hydro machines typically have nonstandard physical footprints when compared to air and immersion machines, and require a suite of advanced racking and cooling systems to operate, but they resemble more common deployments in the mature data center industry.

Hydro mining, like immersion, is a pricey path to pursue, and comes with one additional caveat—because you are working at the cutting edge of mining technology, you are always buying your mining systems from the earliest-stage companies. This can be a risky strategy when deploying hundreds of thousands (if not millions) of dollars in capital expenses.

It should not be assumed that the future of mining will converge towards a single type of cooling. While hydro and immersion cooling are more efficient than air cooling, they incur different costs, require different maintenance schedules, and are optimal for different business models. It's the same way Costco selling a $1.50 hot dog and soda hasn't put Nathan's Famous, Lucky Dogs, or the guy hawking footlongs at the ballpark out of business. It would be naïve to expect a single system or metric such as cooling type or heat transfer coefficient to singularly direct the industry.

Putting the Pieces Together and Starting the Engine

We've introduced the four parts of a Bitcoin miner: the power supply unit, the control board, the hashboard, and the cooling system. With it fully assembled, there are three physical connections required for every Bitcoin miner to operate: a source of electricity, a connection to the internet, and a method of physically cooling the machine. The electrical connection plugs into the power supply unit and the ethernet cable plugs into your control board. Cooling operates via one of the three previously mentioned mechanisms: air, liquid immersion, or hydro cooling.

Congratulations!

With a source of electricity to power the machine, a way for the brain of the machine to communicate to the internet, and a working cooling system, you'll be mining Bitcoin in no time. If you've been reading closely, you'll note that this setup only applies to air-cooled machines. If we were mining Bitcoin using hydro or immersion-cooled machines, we would still be setting up our liquid, pump, and tank systems (more on that later).

Thus far we have focused on the *what* of Bitcoin mining— the necessary pieces, how they are arranged, and the roles they play in the operation of the machine. It's a moderately technical but necessary step in understanding the *how* and *why* of operating these machines. Every operational or business choice a Bitcoin miner makes fundamentally reduces to the four parts of their Bitcoin miner. We'll spend a bit more time in technicalities to apprehend what happens when the machine turns on, what exactly it's doing, and then turn our attention outward from the machine to explore the world around us.

As a general principle, whether you are running a single machine or a fleet of machines, you should always think of operations as if you were a Formula 1 race team. Instead of getting around a track as quickly as possible, your goal is to generate as much work (measured in terahash) as profitably as possible (of course, you should execute this feat without blowing anything up).

In an F1 race, the driver doesn't only press the accelerator. They must also use the brakes to avoid running off the sides of the track in the turns. When the track is cold, wet, or dusty, the race team must strategize around vehicle setup, tuning, and pit strategy to maximize speed under various conditions. In the same way, our Bitcoin miner can't simply consume as much electricity as possible at all points in time. They are beholden to factors outside of their control: temperature shifts over the day or season, elevation and humidity changes that impact machine performance, and even variations in the main input—electricity. Sometimes the electricity or energy isn't there when they want it, and other times it's priced too high for them to profitably consume.

Like the F1 team, the Bitcoin miner is focused on both the technical elements of their task as well as the strategic and business aspects. Like racing, the game of Bitcoin mining is extremely competitive, but instead of chasing after fractions of a second and first place podiums, miners are chasing after marginal efficiencies in J/T, efficient business models, and an asset that grows ever scarcer as the industry fills with more operators. And to top it off, we need to remember that the protocol itself decreases the total issuance of Bitcoin approximately every four years by half.

Those three necessary physical connections—an ethernet cable, an electrical plug, and a method of cooling—are our gateway to understanding machine strategy, incentives, and the resulting businesses that emerge. So, we begin with the internet connection first and what exactly our Bitcoin miner is working on.

The Internet Connection

The humble ethernet connection.

In an age of wireless digital connection, the ethernet cable generally hides, unobtrusively, in your home between your modem and router. It is the last link between the wired and digital age for internet users who have very little understanding of networks, routers, IP addresses, or subnets. Fortunately for us, we don't need to understand the ins and outs of networking to understand

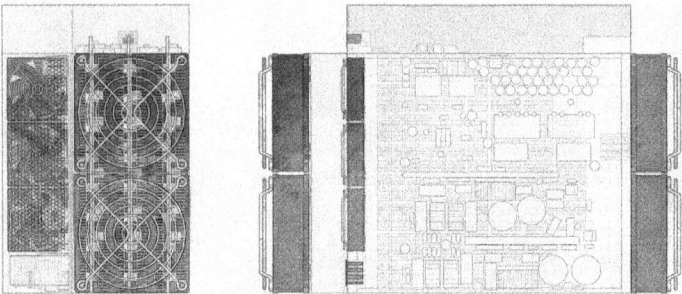

Figure 6: *The three physical connections of a Bitcoin miner: Internet, electricity, and a method of cooling.*

how the machine works and communicates. It is enough to explore just what that ethernet connection allows us to do practically.

The ethernet cable connects to the control board of the Bitcoin miner. It is what allows you to monitor directly what the machine is doing, and it lets the machine connect to your pool or to your node and the Bitcoin network directly to create and submit new blocks. Whether you have a single machine operating in your basement or 10,000 machines in an industrial warehouse, every machine must be networked to a local network and eventually the open internet. Why is that? Because unless we are connected to the network, we cannot receive a reward for the work we perform.

What exactly *is* that work, though?

Before we dive into this topic, let me reassure readers that this is as technical as this book will get (and as close as we will fly to the sun of shadowy super coding). Frankly, I studied philosophy as an undergraduate, and the last thing I want is 400 computer science majors leaving passive-aggressive reviews and walloping me for syntax errors they haven't made since middle school. But suppose we intend to appreciate and explore the business models of Bitcoin mining and the future this industry holds. In that case, we must spend just a little time in the technical weeds grasping how Bitcoin mining works to contribute to the overall network. Then, with that under our belts and our brains approximately 7% larger, we can return to the fun stuff—surviving in this ever-competitive industry and keeping our screaming cyber hornets happy.

BITCOIN MINING IS NOT SOLVING COMPLEX MATH PROBLEMS

The average Bitcoiner works hard to get their 10,000 hours of learning, become competent enough to run a node, set up a secure wallet, and take custody of their Bitcoin. However, when it comes to understanding and explaining Bitcoin mining, an icy glaze rolls over their eyes, and they are compelled to utter the phrase all Bitcoin miners loathe: "Well, you see, the miners are securing the network by solving complex math problems." More superstitious Bitcoin miners say that every time someone invokes "complex math problems," an S19 overheats. (Ok, nobody says this, but it would explain quite a bit about the industry today.)

In truth, Bitcoin miners serve two core functions for the Bitcoin network that assist network security—facilitating transactions and issuing new Bitcoin (also known as the block reward).[16] Bitcoin miners facilitate transactions on the network by building a "block" out of the transactions in the mempool. If you remember your Bitcoin 101, that's where you send your signed transaction with your attached fee to be picked up by a miner, added to a block, and included on the blockchain. The Bitcoin miner then *hashes* that proposed block, using a bit of cryptographic magic called the SHA-256 algorithm, outputting a value they hope fulfills the network difficulty, allowing them to add their block to the Bitcoin network blockchain.

The SHA-256 algorithm is a set of instructions that allows a user to input data, process it via the mathematical rules of the SHA-256 algorithm, then output a unique 'hash' of that data. Regardless of how much data you put in, the hash of the data will always be 64 characters long (for my technical friends, we will not be going down a 32-bit rabbit hole). Moreover, should you change anything in your input data at all, you will output an *entirely different* hash value.

While you may input any kind of data in any kind of order into the SHA-256 algorithm and get a unique hash as the output, what makes the SHA-256 algorithm so special is that you cannot take an output hash and work backward to the original input. The math only "maths" in one direction. Using this SHA-256 algorithm, your input data is 100% verifiable by someone with the original data and the hash. This keeps users of SHA-256 safe from tampering or reverse engineering of data.

More practically, imagine you have a magic SHA-256 wood-chipper, and anything you put into that magic woodchipper emerges on the other side as a totally unique 8-inch by 8-inch box. Put a single human hair in, and your SHA-256 wood chipper spits out a unique 8-inch by 8-inch box. Put a mature black Angus in, and your machine kicks out a different unique 8-inch by 8-inch box. Put a three bedroom/four bath Italian villa in, and you get a different unique 8-inch by 8-inch box.

At this point I imagine visions of the movie Fargo are popping up in your forebrain. Good. You're also hopefully realizing there are conveniences to this machine. For one, everything you put in comes out in a totally unique form that does not resemble the input. Additionally, regardless of the size of your input, you get the same size output. This magical machine allows you to keep your prize black Angus untampered with and easily transportable.

Of course this machine doesn't do us much good in the *real world*. I prefer my Italian villa to stay an Italian villa and not lose the ability to be converted back into a summer home for use. In practice, it's only in the world of data that the SHA-256 algorithm shines.

Consider the following. I want to send my wife a digital birthday card, but I want to be sure her little brother, a prankster, doesn't intercept my message and make me look silly in front of her. I compose the following message: "My Love, To many more years around the sun with my favorite person. Love, Robert." I run this message through the SHA-256 algorithm and it returns the following hash:

b86d6ea046232d4480d552ea83e10555606af 48b953aae8651a959f2a7cfa408.

I then send my wife the e-card as well as that hash. When my wife receives the card, she then independently runs that data through the SHA-256 algorithm, and uh-oh, it returns a hash of:

fb63e8827b7e057acd733dfa47c41ec4b1e088fed3ea e010cda7c5529a3d8708.

The hashes don't match. And what's more, she finds it a bit odd that I would send her a card that says, "My Love, To many more years around the sun with my smelliest person. Love, Robert."

It's a silly example but illustrates the utility of this SHA-256 machine. Any change in your input data will radically change the output hash. Should my original message change by only one letter—say by adding an extra "o" to the word "To"—the output hash again changes drastically:

36bf634f12c368ee7727f32cf9cd0d77c083f4e6963eb 1deff5e9f77003f031a.

The SHA 256 algorithm proves useful in validating data to ensure it hasn't been tampered with while securing it perfectly for sharing. In Bitcoin, rather than hashing birthday messages to family, miners are hashing data that consists of a body and a header organized into a single chunk. This is what we refer to as a block, and as those blocks are formed and organized over time, they form what we call the blockchain. The body of a block consists of the transactions that users submit to the mempool to be finalized and added to the blockchain. The header consists of organizational and reference data such as Bitcoin version, the hash of the previous block, Merkle root hash, time, difficulty, and something called a nonce.[17]

As you can imagine, things in block-building land get very technical very quickly. (I warned you. Stop and get a drink at this point if you need a moment for processing.) We will focus on what is most important for our purposes—the hash of the previous block, the nonce, difficulty, and transactions (apologies to Ralph Merkle for going no deeper, even though you gave us the Merkle root).[18]

The previous block's hash is simply the long string of values formed from running the block header through the SHA-256 algorithm. For example, the hash of the block while writing this section is:

0000000000000000000014f161e726b342f8b56085accf
5205606c56e0ddd3242

also known as block 814,614.[19] Using this hash as part of the data input to our next block, which we then hash using SHA-256 all over again, is what verifiably links one block to the next, forming the blockchain we know and love. Each block is linked to the prior block by the hashing work that has gone into it, and the block that comes next in the future is verifiably linked to the current block by the work that goes into it. But what do we precisely mean when we say *work*?

We know a Bitcoin mining machine is hashing using the SHA-256 algorithm, so why can't it simply hash all of the block header information and submit it for addition to the blockchain immediately? In practice this would cause blocks to pop out every which way from every mining machine across the Earth. Every miner would scoop up transactions and their fees and hash away to win a block reward. Bitcoin issuance would race towards the 21 million cap, and the market would be flooded with miners rapidly inflating the circulating supply of Bitcoin. To avoid this tragic fate, Satoshi introduced the additional design elements of proof-of-work, the nonce, and difficulty. Note, Satoshi did not *invent* these concepts, but rather applied them from various other big-brain cypherpunks and thinkers as elements of the system that is Bitcoin.[20]

As the Bitcoin whitepaper explains, "The proof-of-work involves scanning for a value that when hashed, such as with SHA-256, the hash begins with a number of zero bits. The average work required is exponential in the number of zero bits required and can be verified by executing a single hash… To compensate for increasing hardware speed and varying interest in running nodes over time, the proof-of-work difficulty is determined by a moving average targeting an average number of blocks per hour. If they're generated too fast, the difficulty increases."[21] (Importantly, when Satoshi says 'node' here, they mean someone running the original Bitcoin software, which used CPU power to execute the SHA-256 algorithm. Today when we say node, we are typically referring to someone running the Bitcoin software to validate blocks and keep a record of the blockchain, not for mining as well.)

There is a lot baked into the above excerpt, and if we revisit the hash of our friend—block 814,614—it can help illuminate what is happening:

> 00000000000000000003aadd601b2e7394f1b7c97
> d0c8779260c1388d656852

Notice the hash of this block has a unique characteristic: it begins with nineteen 0s. Curious. The situation becomes even more curious when I look at the hash of the block immediately preceding or following block 814,614. Block 814,613 has a hash of

> 00000000000000000033121eebad315318e79e58ffc
> 493c345af10168b3e341

and block 814,615 has a hash of

00000000000000000000b630329c9b63217663e1881f
cc91d2a2beeadcb455e6.

Recall above when we ran my birthday message through the SHA-256 algorithm and returned a unique and entirely verifiable hash. If I modify that message in any way, it returns a different hash. This makes sense: I'm putting different data into the machine, so I must return different results. SHA-256 seems so easy: I put in an input, follow the rules of the algorithm, and get a specific and unique output. Where exactly is the *work* Satoshi is referring to and what's going on with all of those 0s? One should also reason that the odds of generating a hash with so many leading 0s is exceptionally low.

This is the magic of block creation and the heart of proof-of-work.

To stop Bitcoin blocks from flooding into the network from every which way and inflating supply too quickly, a miner must hash a block that fulfills the network *difficulty*. You can think of Bitcoin difficulty like a thermostat that runs your heating and cooling to keep your house at a comfortable 72 degrees year-round. Unlike your fancy thermostat, Bitcoin does not run the heating if it gets too cold at night, or turn on the air conditioning if the summer sun is blasting. Rather it is designed to keep found blocks to an average of every ten minutes. It does this by counting how quickly blocks come in over a roughly two-week period, or every 2016 blocks,[22] and assigning a difficulty target (those are the 0s you see) that a miner must hit to achieve the difficulty target. If blocks are coming in too quickly, the network adjusts difficulty upwards to make it harder to find blocks (e.g., you may have to hash a block with 20 leading 0s instead of 19).

And if blocks are coming in too slowly, the network does the opposite and reduces the target difficulty by some number of leading 0s to make finding blocks easier.

But how do we find the output hash that has the proper number of leading 0s?

We know a hash algorithm returns a unique and specific output based on the input data. And we know that it's impossible to guess what an input of a hash was by simply looking at it. To achieve an output that has a certain number of leading 0s, we have to *change* part of our input block data before we hash it. This is where the nonce shows up. A nonce, which is a portmanteau of the phrase "number used only once," is exactly what it sounds like—a number that is inserted into the data prior to hashing that will change the output hash of the block (which will either have the proper number of 0s, or more likely not).[23] Our nonce is of great importance because it is the *only* part of the block the mining machine gets to choose before hashing, and it has to choose *a lot* of these numbers.

A Bitcoin miner may have to hash a block with 100s of different nonces to output a hash with one or two leading 0s. To find three or four they may have to hash millions of nonces into their proposed block. To achieve the difficulty target of today's Bitcoin network, a mining machine has to process hundreds of trillions of hashes with unique nonces *every second* to find a block. Even then, a mining machine may never find a single block in its entire lifetime.

When we say proof-of-work, what we are talking about is *machine work.*

Because there is no way to game the one-way mathematics of the SHA-256 algorithm to know which nonce added to our block header data will give us the desired hash output to achieve our difficulty target, we are forced to follow the only strategy that can ensure we ever find a block. We work as hard as we can inserting a nonce into our data, hashing the block, rejecting it if it doesn't fulfill the difficulty target, then trying again, and again, and again, ad infinitum, or until someone else finds a nonce that fulfills the difficulty target and they win the privilege of adding their block to the Bitcoin blockchain. Then, we start hashing a new block, on top of the one that was just added to the block-chain, and guess nonces all over again.

There is something magnificently Sisyphean about a device that has become hundreds upon hundreds of times more efficient than its predecessors, working continuously throughout the entirety of its useful life, executing a task that can only be accomplished by a strategy of guessing, and never achieving that task because of the exponentially increasing difficulty required to fulfill it. It's poetic. But we're not here for poetry: we're here to mine Bitcoin, so back to the Bitcoin miner and our ethernet connection.

Why Do the Work?

Returning to our humble ethernet connection, we understand the *what* of the Bitcoin miner, but need to touch on the *why* to untangle why anyone would acquire and operate a machine that was likely to never succeed at finding a block. In the earliest days of Bitcoin, it was a collectable or experimental trinket shared among a group of mailing list members interested in an obscure form of computer science. The number of individuals who could deeply apprehend and appreciate the early technical innovation of Bitcoin, as well as the secondary and tertiary monetary and cultural effects it could bring, could fit into a Brooklyn coffee shop with room to spare.

There was an ethos of idealism and curiosity, not raw profit. But profit is what fundamentally drives Bitcoin mining, not idealism or curiosity. As Bitcoin matures into a robust form of peer-to-peer electronic cash, it becomes ever more apparent that the miners, i.e. those creating the digital cash, do it to generate flows of Bitcoin or other forms of income, not merely to ideologically assist in securing the network, as many did in the early days. If you were running Bitcoin throughout 2010, you would have started with the hope that your CPU could find a block and reward you with 50BTC (the block reward in that era). But as the network grew, more individuals began running the software, and more powerful GPUs emerged on the scene. Finding a block became an ever-fleeting accomplishment for an individual miner.

As explained above, the Bitcoin 'thermostat' is the target difficulty and the difficulty adjustment. As more individuals began incrementing on mining hardware technology and finding blocks themselves, blocks came in faster than 10 minutes on average over 2016 block periods. This meant the protocol automatically adjusted the difficulty target upwards, making it harder to find a block to keep block discovery as close to an average of 10 minutes as possible. While good for keeping the network secure and processing transactions in a predictable fashion, this posed a problem for early Bitcoin miners. Where they once found a block or two a week, they were rapidly discovering that the increased competition, improved technology, and the resulting increased difficulty was precipitously dropping their success rate when searching for valid blocks.

Enter Marek Palatinus, AKA Slush.

Many of the early conversations around Bitcoin and Bitcoin mining occurred on the BitcoinTalk website, a forum established by Satoshi Nakamoto in late 2009.[24] Slush was an early registrant, joining the forum at the beginning of November 2010, and soon launched what would become Slush Pool, now Braiins Pool.[25] In his original post preceding the launch of Slush Pool, he identified the problem and his strategy to solve it. As he wrote, "Once people started to use GPU-enabled computers for mining, mining became very hard for other people. I'm on Bitcoin for few weeks and didn't find block yet [sic] (I'm mining on three CPUs)... Join poor CPU miners to one cluster and increase their chance to find a block!..."[26]

By using many miners to collaboratively search for a valid block, this new entity, the pool, behaves like one giant Bitcoin miner, finding more blocks in aggregate than can be found by one small miner working on their own. Additionally, this gives the miner a source of stable income, allowing a miner to smooth out expected revenues over days instead of weeks.

The combination of mining technology improvements and pooled mining added both a performance edge and a financial hedge for operators. While the earliest days of Bitcoin mining barely resembled today's breadbox-style ASIC computers hoovering up thousands upon thousands of continuous watts of electricity, the existence and dynamics of pools operate on these principles, refined over a decade earlier.

Today, pool offerings have expanded dramatically. While the premise is the same—you "point" the work of your machine to the pool and work collaboratively to find valid blocks as a member—pool services have evolved to include ancillary services to lure more hash their way. The largest pool at present, Foundry, offers a suite of enterprise-level services such as exportable data, KYC/AML of pool participants, and even SOC accreditation.[27] These offerings are tailored for the largest miners who must comply with external audits and enhanced financial scrutiny to participate in publicly traded markets.

By contrast, pools such as Luxor, Braiins, or Lincoin have chosen different trajectories when developing and offering services to miners. Luxor has worked to develop a Hashprice Index, financial derivatives, and aftermarket firmware to allow for fine machine control and tuning.[28] Braiins offers firmware that increases machine performance and when used allows you to avoid all fees as part of their pool.[29] Lincoin is exploring the energy sector and developing an intelligence suite to enhance operational automation.[30]

Some pools require registration with a verified name and government ID, while others allow you to hash with only an email address. Some pools only reward miners once an actual block is found (referred to as PPLNS) and others pay a miner continuously based on the amount of hash they contribute (referred to as FPPS).[31] Each of these options will appeal to different miners of different scales and business models. There is not necessarily a single *best* pool, but only the best pool for a given miner based on their business model and goals.

It's thanks to the humble ethernet connection that the individual machine is able to participate in this magnificent game of guessing for a profit, and it is thanks to that same ethernet connection that tens if not hundreds of thousands of machines can work collaboratively via pooled mining to stabilize their revenues and more easily plan and grow their operations.

The Electrical Plug

While an ethernet connection is what gains a miner glory on the Bitcoin network, but it is the electrical plug that links the miner to the physical world. As we explore this second connection, we move from the digital realm of networks, hashes, and pools into the material domains of commodities, energy generation, grids, and curtailable load. Where the ethernet cable facilitates miner support for the Bitcoin network, the electrical plug facilitates participation in local commerce, electrical price stability (or even price reduction), and ancillary services rendered to local communities.

How a Bitcoin miner acquires and manages the electricity they use to power their machines is often the determining factor in the success of their business model. While the pool you choose to hash with is unlikely to make or break your bottom line, mismanaging your electricity can kill your company before you plug in a single machine. But before we talk about price per kWh, curtailment, and transformers, we should understand a more fundamental question: *Where does electricity come from?* To answer this question, we will start with the high-level world of energy and work our way down to the electrical plug.

ENERGY

To begin, we'll introduce a simple but powerful idea: Energy is not electricity.

As laypeople, we use the terms energy and electricity interchangeably, but they refer to distinct concepts and give different insights into how one would operate a Bitcoin mining operation

Figure 7: *Examples of common sources of energy: Nuclear, oil, gas, solar, and wind.*

successfully (and most of our modern world for that matter). When we refer to energy, we are referring to the raw resources that, among other things, *may* be used to produce electricity. Energy is in the food you consume, the sun rays on your back-yard garden, or the gasoline in the tank of the mail truck that drops off your packages.

The raw energy resources used to produce the electricity our Bitcoin miner consumes can come in the form of coal, oil, natural gas, nuclear rods, water, wind and the sun. We take these raw energy sources and convert them into consumable electric-ity by burning, boiling water, spinning a large wind or water turbine, or utilizing various other piezoelectrics, heating, and engineered rotation methods. This applies to every electrified device we use. The modern world runs on electricity, and we need a lot of it.

We refer to those various mechanisms that convert raw resources into usable electricity as generators. No Bitcoin mining machine can run without some form of generation (if you do find a way of running a Bitcoin miner without a generator, please contact me immediately!). Once we grasp that various raw materials are converted into usable electricity via generators, we can introduce another important entity—the grid.

While there is energy in the sun, the wind, a barrel of oil, a ton of coal, or a nuclear rod, that energy is not evenly distributed or equally abundant throughout the world. You'd be hard-pressed to find a coal miner in South Florida, or a large solar farm operator in Northern Maine. Contrarily, Northern Wyoming, sitting on one of the world's largest reserves of high grade coal, has ample coal miners and coal plants throughout the Powder River Basin generating electricity. Likewise, Southern California, Arizona, and Nevada host some of the largest solar arrays in the United States.[32]

Energy is all around us, but the ability to convert it into usable electricity depends on how easy it is to acquire locally or transport to a consumer. Coal, nuclear rods, and oil and gas are highly transportable and can be sent via rail, truck, or pipeline to a generator to be converted into electricity. Compare that convenience to a solar array, wind farm, or hydroelectric dam. Optimal locations for these electrical generators are where the sun shines abundantly and wind blows or water flows continuously. Even then, the sun, wind, and water vary in abundance by day and season. Electricity produced in one region can be transported long distances via high-voltage power lines, but there are substantial upfront costs to building these large projects, and over long enough distances up to 6% of the total electricity transmitted can be lost to heat.[33]

The governmental response to these factors within the United States, combined with federal initiatives to distribute consistent and affordable electricity across the country, is the development of Regional Transmission Organizations and Independent System Operators (RTOs and ISOs, respectively).[34] These organizations, overseen by the semi-governmental Federal Energy Regulatory Commission (FERC), work to ensure consistent and affordable electricity for consumers.[35] These RTOs and ISOs operate within nine distinct geographic regions[36] and work with every generator, be they solar, wind, coal, or nuclear, to ensure consistent delivery of affordable power to end consumers.[37]

When we refer to "the grid," we are most often conceptualizing the direct link from the plugs in the walls of our homes through various under and overground wires to some distant but not too far away source of generation. If you're a Telsa-driving nouveau-riche yuppie, you imagine delicate sun rays powering your vehicle from some idyllic solar farm. If you're a West Texas wildcatter, you flip on the lights and glory in the combined-cycle natural gas turbine sending AC current to your front door. We almost never consider the system—the high-level schema of assorted generators of various types and sizes scattered tens or hundreds of miles away from us. Even less frequently do we consider the ISO, RTO, or other regional or local market structure that coordinates those generators to produce and deliver affordable and reliable electricity for end consumers like you and me.

THE MIX

The supply of the electricity we power our lives with every day is an ever-changing mix of sun, wind, coal, gas, water, and nuclear radiation. However, over the course of any given day, the demand on those generators and the grid operator varies widely. At 3 a.m. a sleeping community needs less electricity than at 7 p.m. when they're huddled around the television or computer watching old episodes of *The Office*. This change in demand over the course of a day is often referred to as the duck curve. Don't ask me why—I don't think it looks like a duck at all—but the name stuck, and that's what we call the load curve over a 24-hour period.[38]

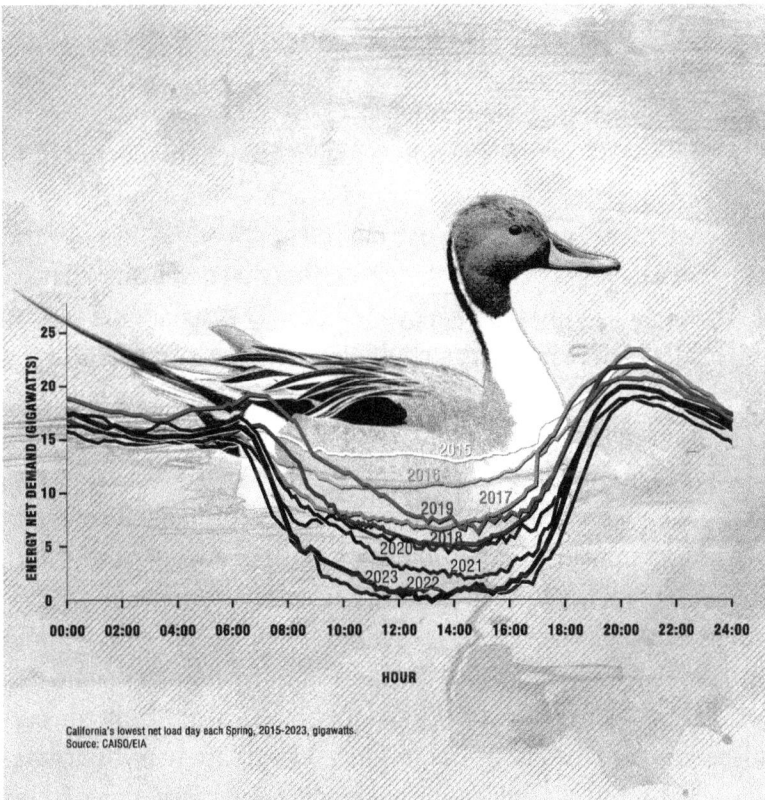

Figure 8: *The Duck Curve*

The duck curve creates an interesting set of problems for our grid operator. The supply of electricity must always match the demand, because at present, grid-scale energy storage does not exist. So a grid operator does what they must to keep the lights on: they estimate the upcoming demand for electricity based on factors such as season, weather, the types of consumers they are serving, and a variety of additional factors (likely including wizardry). They then coordinate with electrical generators, typically via a market mechanism of bidding for production at particular hours, to match the demand for electricity with supply.

You would think this is the ideal solution, but a difficult game is only beginning.

Because generators use free market mechanisms to bid to produce electricity over the course of a day, this should ensure that customers are always receiving the most competitive electric rates, regardless of where their electricity comes from (that's a fancy way of saying the cheapest electricity is what gets sent to the grid). However, the reality of electrical generation throws a monkey wrench into grid operator plans for a beautifully balanced grid. Electrical generators are not all created equal.

Recall our main sources of energy from above—coal, oil, natural gas, nuclear, water, wind, and the sun (if I've left out your favorite pet project like biomass or geothermal, stay with me; this is a book on Bitcoin mining, not a dissertation on grids). Some of these forms of electricity are dispatchable, and some are non-dispatchable. (That means you can call them up and ask for more or less power if you need it.) Some are intermittent, and some are continuous. Some produce electricity near their total nameplate capacity, while others only produce a fraction of their overall capacity (a metric known as capacity factor).

When a grid operator is working to make supply match demand day in and day out, they think of the grid in terms of the types of load at their disposal. Baseload is electricity from large, continuously operating plants that provide a reliable backstop. Load following or intermediate loads, such as combined-cycle gas plants, can ramp up or down throughout the day to meet consumer needs as demand varies. And finally, there are peaker plants, such as open-cycle gas turbines, that ramp up extremely quickly in times of spiking demand.

Add to this equation the difference between dispatchable and non-dispatchable loads. You can call a peaker plant and have more production on your grid in 20 minutes. You can't do the same to a wind farm or solar array. A nuclear plant can very confidently tell you how much electricity they will be able to produce for the grid tomorrow, the next month, or the next five years. A wind farm—not so much. The dispatchability of a generator, as well as the intermittent or continuous production of that generator, informs a metric we call capacity factor—namely, how much electricity does a generator produce relative to their actual nameplate production capacity. This number is typically represented as a percentage and can be thought of in the same way one might think of hotel bookings. If you own a 200-room hotel and keep every room filled every day of the year, you would be operating at 100% capacity factor. If you're only able to fill 100 rooms per night over the course of a year, your capacity factor will drop to 50%. In short, capacity factor is the metric that allows you to measure the extent to which a generator uses all of their revenue-producing resources to their fullest capacity.

Strong, stable, and predictable nuclear energy has an incredibly high capacity factor, ranging in the 80s and 90s. This means a nuclear facility with a nameplate capacity of 1 gigawatt of energy, or 1,000 megawatts, is consistently producing power in the 800 to 900 megawatt range over a given period. Compare that to a wind farm with the same 1 gigawatt installed capacity. You can expect to consistently operate at a capacity factor between 20% and 40%, producing around 200 to 400 megawatts of energy over a given period.[39] These capacity factors suggest that to produce the same amount of energy from a wind farm as a nuclear plant in a given year, you would have to triple or quadruple the size of your wind farm.

Loads such as nuclear, geothermal, coal, and some gas turbines have relatively high-capacity factors and some degree of dispatchability. This allows a grid operator to utilize them for baseload production in order to ensure there is always some minimum electrical load available to consumers, and with the appropriate foresight, to ramp those loads up and down in response to grid demand. Loads such as wind, solar, some hydropower, and other flavors of gas turbine and combustion peaker plants vary widely in their dispatchability and intermittence. I can call up a peaker plant to deliver 50MW to my grid. I can't do the same with my solar arrays on a rainy day. What's more, when it's sunny the following day, my solar plants are going to sell all of their available electricity to the market, which can create price crashes and spikes as baseload and intermediate load respond to the changing glut of electricity on the grid.

The grid operator has a tall task, and should you ever have the pleasure of meeting one, you should thank them abundantly for helping to keep your lights on at home.

Their mandate is to provide ample electricity at a reasonable rate to consumers, and they must do so while working to maintain

Figure 9: *An illustration of a large hydroelectric dam, often a high-capacity factor source of electricity.*

an open market for electrical generators without introducing unnecessary risks to the grid. The risks vary widely depending on who you ask, but one emergent trend in the developed world is becoming clear. Most first-world consumers think of the electrical grid from an environmentalist perspective, not from a human flourishing perspective.[40] This has led to aggressive advocacy against carbon-emitting forms of generation like coal and natural gas, often at the expense of reliable and cost-effective electrical production.

When most people in the developed world are asked if they would like to build more solar arrays and battery banks to generate electricity and help save the whales, they tend to agree immediately. A grid operator, dealing with the actual day-to-day task of delivering load to consumers, sees an emerging risk factor: a non-dispatchable load that produces most of its electricity during midday, out of sync when most consumers are using electricity. In fact, solar electricity is rapidly disappearing into the sunset when most people are getting home from work and consuming the most electricity they will use for the day.[41] And I haven't even mentioned the immense utilization of hydrocarbons to manufacture, deliver, and install those electrical generators—and the geopolitical risks tied to lithium and cobalt production.[42]

By comparison, rapidly developing nations like China are building forms of electrical generation that most reliably power their citizens (woe to the whales). In fact, as of 2022, new construction starts on coal power capacity in China were six times larger than the rest of the world combined.[43] (Remember that the next time you see an undergraduate poly-science major with pink bangs gluing themselves to a road in Essex or throwing paint on a Monet in the Met. They're advocating in the wrong neighborhood.)

Think of the electrical generators of all types. Each of those producers is a discrete business, and they want to sell their product to the market at a profit. Each of those producers has startup costs and continued costs of operation, whether they stem from putting coal on a train, gas into a pipeline, or tapping the energy on a sunny or windy day. They necessarily must turn a profit to survive.

When you consider that the grid needs reliable and well-priced energy, and the generators on that grid need to profitably produce and distribute as much electricity as they can, you begin to understand why a Bitcoin miner is a welcome participant in this arrangement. They are an ideal customer, hungry to consume as much electricity as possible, sensitive to the cost of electricity, and can turn off in seconds or minutes when desired. While your typical electrical consumer will leave the air conditioning on when it's 108 degrees out or keep the foundry burning so as not to ruin tens of tons of raw materials, a Bitcoin miner will quite happily curtail their demand when it becomes unprofitable to keep consuming electricity and generating hashes.

Waste and Bitcoin Mining Part I

We have familiarized ourselves with various players on the electrical grid—the generators and operators who participate in the complex dance of continuously balancing supply and demand of electrical load to ensure you and I can keep our iPhones on 100% and our tweets going out. This overview is a simple conceptualization of one of the most complex machines humanity has built, but aims to make you comfortable enough with the grid to appreciate both the complexities of grid operation as well as potential opportunities for activities like Bitcoin mining that feasts on abundant electricity.

We began this section with a simple distinction: energy is not electricity. With this understanding, we can appreciate how various raw materials, coal, oil, natural gas, nuclear rods, water, wind, or the sun, and their availability and readiness to be converted into usable electricity on the consumer grid. But to fully appreciate how Bitcoin miners interact with their main input, electricity, we must take one step backward from the grid and dig deeper into those sources of energy and electrical generators directly, whether or not they are attached to a grid.

To do so we introduce a second distinction: namely that while energy cannot be created or destroyed, *it can be wasted*. The whole of the energy supply chain, from raw commodities to electrical generation to grid and transmission to customers, consists of various energy businesses all competing to operate profitably. Each of those businesses, like all businesses, generate waste. That waste exists in many forms, but most simply the waste is energy and electricity that is inefficiently used, or energy for which there is no demand.

Energy that is sub-optimally used is akin to driving your car driving down the highway versus trudging along in stop-and-go traffic. An engine moving a two-ton vehicle in the latter is far less efficient at using gas when compared to a cross-country trip on cruise control at 70 miles per hour. Energy lacking demand may be in the form of trapped hydrocarbons in a well, too far from a pipeline to be economically usable, or a grid-connected wind farm that idles turbines in the middle of the day because demand is too low. This becomes wasted energy, and wasted energy is lost revenues for producers of commodities and generators of electricity.

Said another way, using energy inefficiently or having an energy supply with no consumer both create waste. This seems counterintuitive to the modern electrical consumer. How can energy be lacking in efficient production or demand? Don't we live in the 21st century?!

Figure 10: *An illustration of a behind the meter Bitcoin mining farm, co-located with a source of generation.*

When you compare the increase in fuel energy supply between 1971 and 2019, you find that the total amount has grown more than 2.5 times, from 230 to 630 exajoules.[44] This should be expected. The population of the Earth grew from an estimated 3.77 billion to 7.76 billion over the same period of time, reflecting a more than two fold growth in population.[45] These numbers indicate the amount of energy supply has grown faster than total population growth, which suggests that humanity *really likes using energy in their daily lives.* If this is the case, it wouldn't seem obvious that a massive amount of energy is wasted, but a substantial amount is. This isn't only when utilizing sources of primary energy via raw materials like natural gas, coal, petroleum, or biomass, but also during the process of conversion into usable electricity and transmission to a final consumer.

In fact, research suggests that approximately 66% of the energy we consume is rejected energy, or energy released back into the environment in the form of heat.[46] Looking only at the US electrical grid, federal data suggests approximately 60% of raw energy is lost in the process of conversion into usable electricity, also in the form of heat. You may be as surprised as I was at discovering these fun facts for the first time (the same sort of surprise as finding out you will have to pay taxes for the rest of your natural life or risk a financial colonoscopy from the IRS). But energy loss is a law of the universe, not a law of mankind. In fact we have a name for it—the Second Law of Thermodynamics.[47]

Inefficiency during raw energy conversion into work is nothing revolutionary, yet it provides an opportunity for the aspiring Bitcoin miner. All electrical generators, akin to the engine in your car, have an optimal operational speed and a peak efficiency at which they can convert a raw energy source into electricity.

Ignoring non-dispatchable generators like our windmills and solar arrays for a moment, natural gas plants, coal plants, and nuclear plants, want to hum along and output the most efficient amount of MW per hour relative to their size and inputs. This is driving with cruise control on—65 miles per hour gets you 28 miles per gallon, and any faster or slower and you only get 27 miles per gallon. When you hit traffic in Indianapolis on that road trip and crawl past Lucas Oil Stadium at 3 miles per hour, you're probably only getting 18 miles per gallon—a substantial loss in efficiency.

In the same way, an electrical generator delivering megawatts to a grid may be called to vary its output in response to consumer demand (remember the duck curve). But unlike a car hitting traffic and decelerating to avoid rear-ending the car in front of them, a generator has a new resource at their disposal: the Bitcoin miner. The Bitcoin miner provides dispatchable base demand to the generator or grid operator. They are ready and willing, for a price, to ramp up and consume their excess electricity or ramp down when Gladys needs her AC at 64 during a hot Texas summer (stay cool Gladys). This source of steady but flexible demand improves efficiency at the level of the generator as well as the grid itself. We'll explore these business models in greater depth in the following sections and leave the problem of generator efficiency and thermodynamics to the engineers.

WASTE AND BITCOIN MINING PART II

The second form of energy waste is energy without demand, and it comes in a few key flavors. It appears odd to discuss energy without demand in a world where per capita energy consumption is increasing. Yet, energy lacking demand occurs for a variety of reasons. Generators may produce energy at times when energy is not needed, or they may have immense amounts of energy too far away from a consumer to incentivize transport to a market.

The first example of wasted energy and electrical production when it isn't needed is a defining feature of non-dispatchable, variable renewable energies such as solar and wind. In our prior exploration of the duck curve, we found a disconnect between the rising of the sun, the blowing of the wind, and the consumption of energy. When most individuals wake up, turning on their lights, toasters, and coffeemakers to go to work, the sun barely scratches the horizon and the wind isn't yet blowing at full force. By the time most individuals are deep into their working day, electrical production is soaring, but consumption has leveled out or has potentially dropped.

This mismatch between supply and demand leads to an over-supply of variable renewable energies like wind and solar. The effect on the grid is substantial. There are even portions of the central United States in the Southwest Power Pool ISO where *electrical prices are negative* in excess of 25% of the time over the course of a year.[48] States like Kansas and Oklahoma, with sub-stantial wind farms, produce over 47% of their electricity from wind.[49] However, wind is variable, and these States find them-selves oversupplying during times of low or moderate demand and high production. Additionally, the grid can only facilitate so much transmission at once. There are hard limits to how much electricity you can put on the wires and through the transformers that eventually deliver it to your home or business, and energy congestion emerges in times of high production.

What is less intuitive is how electrical pricing can go neg-ative. One would think oversupply and transmission capacity would bid down prices to free and no further, but the addition of renewable energy credits or tax credits for carbon-free electrical production allow generators to pay to deliver their electricity to the grid and still make a profit.

For example, imagine you operate a pizza shop in Detroit across the street from your nearest competitor. Your competitor makes Detroit-style pizza with ingredients sourced from a big box store. But you, a pizza artist, make Detroit-style pizza with seasonal ingredients from local farmers who cut deals for you to see their ingredients in a local shop. In truth, customers can't seem to taste the difference between either pizza, and they cost about the same to make, so demand splits equally between street corners. Heck, you and your competitor even charge the same prices for your pizzas!

One day you get a bright idea. If the customers can't tell the difference in taste, you're going to charge a dollar less for your pies to improve demand. You drop the price and watch customers flood into your restaurant for the day. But to your horror, the next day your competitor has dropped their price to match yours! Again, you drop the price a dollar and watch customers rush to your storefront, only to be matched by your competitor the next day. This goes on for a full week until you are charging the cost of ingredients for your pizza and no more. It's not clear how this price war can continue and anyone will be able to pay rent or employees, but you have a secret you're about to unveil.

The mayor came to your storefront a few months ago and loved your focus on locally sourced Detroit pizza that empowers small business suppliers. She declared your shop a "Designated Cultural Steward for Detroit," which gave you a 15% reduction on your sales and property taxes and made you eligible for a grant that comes out to ~$2 per pizza.

With this ace up your sleeve, you continue the price war, dropping your price *below* your

cost of ingredients. Customers again flood in, but when you wake up the following day, your competitor has failed to match your price. They can go no lower. While you can sell under your cost of production and still make a profit on the tax rebate and grant, your competitor, having achieved no preferential status with the city, finds themselves unable to sell their product at a loss and compete with you in the market.

This example of variable renewable energy and price wars during times of high production and low demand details how electrical generation at the wrong time can drive prices to zero and below. But time is not the only factor contributing to the value of electricity. As your real estate agent knows better than most, location, location, location is a key element in generating and delivering electricity at a profit. A second example of wasted energy and electricity is akin to being a nice house in the wrong neighborhood.

There are two predominant ways energy finds itself stranded in the wrong neighborhood—overbuilt electrical production in low-demand areas and reserves of energy resources without proximity to a market. While these sound the same, they differ in that the first is a function of overbuilt electrical generation, while the second is a function of excess *energy* availability.

Our first example is the Itaipu Dam on the border of Paraguay and Brazil, blocking the Parana River which divides the countries. The dam lies just North of Ciudad del Este in Paraguay and Foz do Iguaçu in Brazil. It may surprise you to hear that this dam, on a river you've never heard of just north of two cities you've never been to, houses (at 14 gigawatts of capacity) the third largest hydroelectric generating plant on the face of the Earth.[50]

This massive hydroelectric undertaking was the result of prolonged multi-country negotiations beginning in 1966, followed by treaty writing and eventual ratification between Paraguay, Brazil, and even Argentina (Why? Because of their real fear of someone using the dam as a weapon and flooding Buenos Aires during a moment of political malice or incompetence). Negotiations were prolonged and included various conditions of ownership and operation, most famously Annex C, which indicated that while Paraguay was entitled to 50% of the electricity produced from the dam, they were not entitled to do with their electricity as they pleased.[51]

Negotiations were followed by an official groundbreaking in 1971 and project completion a whopping 13 years later in 1984. Over 40,000 individuals, mostly recruited from Brazil, would build a series of dams 4.8 miles long and up to 738 feet high to install a total of twenty 700 MW hydroelectric turbines.[52] The rated capacity of this modern marvel is 14 gigawatts, but due to the treaty with Argentina, only 18 of the 20 total installed units are allowed to run at any one point in time (to keep Buenos Aires above water).

Imagine you and your neighbor own adjoining lots in a beautiful and rural stretch of Iowa. You want to build a baseball diamond for your kids to play on and realize the perfect location is an open field bisected by the lot line. One weekend afternoon you bring up the idea of a baseball diamond to your neighbor, and they think it's brilliant. You both decide to allocate personal resources and build a beautiful baseball diamond with the property line running right over home plate and across the pitcher's mound.

But before the first pitch is thrown, you decide it would be wise to sit down with your neighbor and sort out the details of baseball diamond operations. You agree that you both have access to the diamond 50% of the time. You mention that your family is much smaller than your neighbors. You have two kids, while your pal across the road has five, all of whom play baseball and softball competitively. You are interested in potentially generating some revenue from your time with the baseball diamond, maybe renting it out to local teams or community groups looking for a nice location to hone their skills.

It is then your good pal across the road gets a little quiet. You know, he says, he's always loved how rural this stretch of Iowa is, and he couldn't imagine all of those cars racing up and down the road, not to mention the space needed for extra parking and the subsequent mess in the fields during summer rainstorms. For the sake of the baseball diamond, he couldn't possibly agree to such a plan. But, you know, he has five kids, and they're all looking for a little bit more time to practice. What if he were to *rent* the baseball diamond from you? (At a steep discount of course, because you're neighbors after all.)

This is where problems begin for Paraguay. While they are entitled to 50% of the energy produced by the dam, they are not entitled to do as they please with the electricity generated. Annex C dictates that Paraguay is not allowed to sell their electricity to corporations or countries *other than* Brazil. Paraguay has approximately 6.9 million people, and the Itaipu Dam provides over 85% of the electricity required for the entire country.[53] Even so, this only accounts for ~20% of their total allocation, which leaves Paraguay to sell much of the remaining 80% back to their neighbor, often at steep discounts.[54] By contrast, Brazil is a country of approximately 217 million people,[55] and the Itaipu Dam provides only ~9% of their total electrical needs.[56] They can easily gobble up the excess electrical capacity, putting Paraguay in a difficult position when it comes to maximizing the use of their rightful resources.

Bitcoin miners serve a unique role for the Paraguayan side of the Itaipu Dam. A large consumer, willing to pay the same or slightly more for electricity than the Brazilian government or large Brazilian corporations, allows Paraguay to fully capitalize on the ownership of their asset and avoid the uncomfortable limitations of Annex C entirely.

The second way energy is wasted due to location is an abundance of energy without proximity to a market. A striking example is the storied "golden asteroid"—a 140-mile-wide chunk of iron, nickel, and gold that orbits our solar system somewhere between Mars and Jupiter. It goes by the name 16 Psyche and is unique enough to have caught the attention of NASA. In fact, they're launching a satellite to study this immense hunk of metal. Some even value this asteroid at $10,000 quadrillion dollars.[57] If this number, larger than the entire economy of our planet, gives you pause, it should.

Putting a monetary value on a space object over five years of travel away from Earth (in one direction, mind you) is an absurd task. While it is true that 16 Psyche, a space El Dorado, actually exists, the feasibility of traveling to and returning home with a chunk of it to sell is nay impossible. Space travel, as measured in the cost to deliver 1lb of payload to low-Earth orbit, has decreased by orders of magnitude since the early 60s. What once cost many hundreds of thousands of dollars per pound of payload can now be transported by a Space X Falcon Heavy rocket for approximately $3,300 per pound.[58]

Even so, launching a mission to travel to 16 Psyche to somehow land, identify, mine, and load materials, then somehow return and land back on Earth to sell them is a ten-year journey with no clear budgetary constraint. Is it worth one hundred million dollars? One billion? One hundred billion dollars? At a certain price point, it becomes clear that neither you, nor I, nor most nation-states or multinational corporations can cut the check to fund this exploration.

The *functional* value of a 140-mile-wide chunk of iron, nickel, and gold is zero. The same is true if it was made entirely of diamonds, or sapphires, or first-edition Beanie Babies. A 140-mile-wide chunk of anything between Jupiter and Mars doesn't have a meaningful monetary value because it has no access to any available market to be priced. It is akin to valuing the total gold in the Rocky Mountains or the sum value of all of the oil in the Middle East. A fun thought experiment a business analyst may perform to predict total market size, but not an immediately actionable metric without picks, shovels, diggers, drill rigs, and most importantly, buyers on the other side of that work.

The giant golden space asteroid is an extreme case of our access to markets problem, but the same principle applies to industries across our world every day, most notably in the oil and gas industry. It influences the wildcatters exploring oil fields in search of minerals, the intermediary businesses that transport and refine those minerals, and you and I, the end consumers. The hunt for and transport of valuable resources is driven by a market pricing mechanism that must remain above zero for the supply chain to work at all.

The complexity of the oil and gas industry is akin to the grid and electrical generation in many ways. While they are directly related by a supply chain, as oil and gas products are often inputs to electrical generators for grid distribution and consumption, they

Figure 11: *An illustration of an oil rig offshore in remote waters.*

also share similarities in their geographic diversity, engineer-heavy workforces, and complex state and federal oversight and regulatory regimes.

To understand our oil and gas problem, we begin by thinking about poking a hole into the ground. Well before we poke anything into the ground, a process of exploration, permitting, and leasing begins far in advance. Oil and gas companies use a variety of tools as diverse as paleontology and seismography to map precisely where to poke their hole. They then work through negotiations with private, state, federal, and/or tribal parties to determine a mix of surface and mineral rights that pay out royalties and the spoils of oil and gas production once a well is successfully drilled.[59] Wells can take 50 to 60 days to drill and another 7 to 40 to complete and prepare for production, but once the hole has been successfully poked into the ground, many wells can produce in excess of 50 years.[60]

Once a well is up and running, it brings one of three things to the surface: oil, natural gas, or associated gas (a mix of both oil and natural gas). These resources are transported to refineries via tankers, pipelines, or even trucks (what is called midstream) and are eventually refined and distributed for final consumption at downstream facilities and even a Costco Gas station near you (love those extendable fuel lines).[61] Oil is a valuable and highly transportable resource that comes in liquid form. You can pump it into a pipeline, put it into large trucks, or fill a seagoing tanker with it and sail it across the ocean. But natural gas, that other resource that emerges from our hole in the ground, creates a new set of operational and environmental issues.

Less valuable than its oil counterpart, natural gas is a bit of a redheaded stepchild in the industry. When you're digging for valuable oil and gas begins to bubble to the surface, you may only find yourself with a few options as an oil and gas operator. Depending on the regulations where you are and what resources you have available to you, you may capture that gas to sell to a nearby pipeline, flare it by setting it on fire, or least desirable, you may vent it directly to the atmosphere. Natural gas, after all, is odorless and colorless. Who will know?

As oil and gas production technology advances and more and more holes are poked into the ground in search of that proverbial money milkshake, natural gas continues to create problems for operators. On one hand, setting your product on fire as soon as you acquire it, or setting it free to wander the atmosphere, is an economically wasteful way to operate. However, it is often the case that associated gas requires the removal of the natural gas to acquire a higher volume of oil production. The more natural gas you can remove, the more oil you can pump.

Then come the environmental issues. Methane emissions are estimated to cause ~30% of all man-made environmental warming and are estimated to be 40 to 70 times as damaging as carbon dioxide, that other climate bogeyman.[62] Whether or not you, as an oil and gas operator, are concerned with burning or venting the products of your labor away, governments and undergraduates who spray orange paint on classic works of art are hellbent on heavily regulating if not altogether banning your industry in the name of an impending Climate Crisis™. This is not to say that natural gas leaks, vents, and flares are not an issue. Annual global methane emissions from all sources are estimated at 348 million tons per year, with the primary generators being agriculture, energy production like oil, gas, and coal, and waste decaying in landfills.[63]

The oil and gas operator has a difficult path to navigate. The market demand for oil and gas products has only continued to rise as more and more of the world modernizes and consumption of electricity, industrial and home products, and commercial uses follow suit. Meanwhile, countries sign climate pledges and politicians give speeches about net zero goals and a world of only renewable energy sources.

While the virtues of natural gas are many—most importantly the incredible efficiency in combustion to generate electricity (not to mention that natural gas has single-handedly kept electrical prices low for Western consumers as coal generation has been slowly regulated out of operation over the last 20 years)—waste in the industry via leaks, venting, and flaring pose discrete risks in a world where gas comes as a byproduct of oil production and policymakers are near-universally condemning the climate impacts.

To make matters worse, while you, a wise oil and gas operator, have chosen to poke your hole in a location with ample supply of minerals and transportation to a market, many operators are not so lucky. Huge volumes of gas are currently stranded, some with wells drilled and some without, with no viable economic pathway to a buyer. This gas may be too far from a pipeline or "sour" with high concentrations of nitrogen or hydrogen sulfide. It may be too technically difficult to acquire (i.e., offshore in the Arctic) or might be regulated out of economic feasibility due to unfriendly local governments. This total volume is on the order of hundreds of trillions of cubic feet of methane.[64] Natural gas exists in abundance, but poke your hole in the wrong location and you may quickly find that you have a giant golden space asteroid all to yourself.

Enter again our friend the Bitcoin miner, a device that only wants to gorge on continuous electricity while helping the network to order blocks and issue new Bitcoin. If these stranded and wasted resources cannot make it to market, maybe there is a solution to bring the market to them? After all, a Bitcoin miner has only three physical connections: an ethernet cable, an electrical plug, and a method of cooling. If you can convert your energy resources into electricity directly on site, surely you can set up a satellite internet connection to communicate with the network. Yet before we discuss the various ways Bitcoin mining contributes to energy industries in our second section, we must complete our exploration of inputs with the third physical machine connection—the cooling mechanism.

Cooling

When running, a Bitcoin miner may consume anywhere from 100s to 1,000s of watt-hours of electricity (that is, electricity over time, which is how most people consume and are billed for electricity). One of the most recognized but dated pieces of mining hardware, the S9, consumes ~1,400Wh. Newer, more efficient versions of machines from manufacturers such as Bitmain and MicroBT consume in excess of 3,000Wh in most air-cooled versions and over 5,000Wh in many immersion and hydro models. As we already know, energy can neither be created nor destroyed, so once it is directed into the machine for hashing, it must go somewhere. That somewhere is in the form of heat, and a lot of it.

Our Bitcoin miner, like most computers, is a device that converts input electricity into output heat at a near one-to-one ratio.[65] If it takes 1,400W to run your S9, you will have to evacuate that same amount of energy in heat. The reasons for this are beyond our current purposes, but it conveniently allows us to plan machine cooling based almost directly on the nameplate operating wattage of a Bitcoin mining machine.

The most common forms of cooling are onboard fans, oil immersion, or specialized hydro systems. To best understand what differentiates one form of cooling from another, there is one core concept to apprehend—the heat transfer coefficient. The heat transfer coefficient is a number that describes how effectively heat moves between a surface and a liquid. The higher the number, the higher degree of heat transference.[66]

Professional engineering dictates that we understand the properties of our heated surface, the hydrodynamic flow of our liquid, and the boundary conditions between the two surfaces to accurately calculate a heat transfer coefficient. However, for our application in the world of Bitcoin mining, the raw differences in the heat transfer coefficients between air, oil, and water are large enough to save us the trouble of pulling out our pencils.

By rough comparison, air cooling can have a heat transfer coefficient range of 5 to 37, oil immersion from 50 to 350, and water from 100 to 1200. (Before my engineering friends pull up their email accounts to write disapproving letters, let me explain; to keep our fluid comparisons as simple as possible, these coefficients are calculated from gas, oil, and water in free convection as $W/(M^2K)$.[67] These ranges differ in orders of magnitude. They express the degree to which a cooling system that relies on a single method of cooling may be optimized and the potential cooling gained by switching to a system with a higher heat transfer coefficient.

To be concrete, imagine a single air-cooled Bitcoin miner on a card table in your backyard. The machine uses powered fans to pull, accelerate, and exhaust air at a high rate of speed through the body of the machine. The ability of this airflow to cool our miner will change based on variables, such as the fan's speed, the fans' size, the air's current ambient temperature, and even our current elevation. An un-optimized air-cooled system may use underpowered fans in a hot environment on a 7,500-foot high mesa in Arizona, while an optimized air-cooled system may use added industrial-sized fans in a temperate or cool geography much closer to sea level. Between these two systems, we can expect better performance from the one that allows a greater volume of high-velocity cool air to pass through the machine. Still, the physics of the system will limit us to a natural ceiling in our heat transfer coefficient of around 37.

Moving to an oil-cooled system improves our heat transfer coefficient substantially. By moving our machine into the equivalent of a recirculating fish tank full of specialized oil, we're able to more than 10x the cooling effectiveness of the system with a heat transfer coefficient that ranges from 50 to 350. The specialized oil we utilize is called dielectric fluid, and is engineered to carry heat away from the working electronics without bursting into flames, electrifying us, or dissolving away parts of the machine.

While an oil-cooled system offers an immediate jump in cooling capability, it also introduces additional system complexity. Instead of a fan moving air across your machine, you now use pumps that push oil through your tank system. Once that oil has passed through the machine and gained temperature, you now have heated oil to deal with. This oil can be sent directly to a dry cooler or radiator system like you would have in your car, or it can be sent through a plate exchanger, which transfers the heat from the oil to another medium, typically water, which can now be cooled by a dry cooler or radiator system.

A plate exchanger is a hunk of metal with a series of channels inside that allows you to pump in two liquids that can transfer heat to each other but never physically touch. Hot oil goes into one set of pathways, while cool water goes through another. The heat from the oil is transferred to the water without the liquids mixing. Cool oil then leaves the plate exchanger to return to the Bitcoin miner for cooling, while the newly hot water is pumped to a dry cooler to be cooled. A system that cools oil directly with a radiator or dry cooler is called a single-loop system, whereas one that uses a plate exchanger and liquid water for cooling is a double-loop system. Exploring the differences between these two setups is beyond our current scope, but suffice it to say that immersion cooling systems work via one of these two mechanisms and both have their own virtues.

The final leap in cooling effectiveness comes in the move from oil immersion to hydro mining. With a heat transfer coefficient of 100 to 1200, water improves upon oil in its ability to uptake and dissipate heat from the machine. However, the physical footprint of the hydro machine often differs substantially from air or immersion units. While air-cooled or dedicated immersion-cooled units are typically designed to move air or oil across the entire machine, hydro units utilize intake and outlet ports to direct water through cooling blocks or channels throughout the body of the machine itself. For this reason, hydro machines are typically sold in conjunction with their cooling systems, including racking, pumps, and often dry coolers. These systems have the benefit of remaining closed to the outside environment, not being as influenced by ambient conditions like air-cooled systems, and are less likely to be fouled like tanks of machines surrounded in recirculating immersion oil.

That being said, it would be incorrect to assume that all mining will gravitate towards hydro mining because physics dictates it has the best cooling dynamics. The cost to set up and the technical expertise needed to run a miner climbs steadily as you move from air cooling to oil immersion and then to hydro mining, and neither the money nor the technical know-how to successfully run these machines exists in abundant quantities today.

Purchasing a fleet of miners is akin to purchasing a vehicle for your family or business. When you go into the dealership or peruse Craigslist, you're never deciding from the set of all cars available for purchase. Rather, you have a budget to spend and a few key traits in mind. If you and your spouse have a new baby, you may be thinking about safety stars and the spaciousness of the backseat. If all you do is commute to and from work five days a week, you likely select a vehicle based on fuel efficiency. And if you're about to start that lawn care and snow plowing business you've been talking about for years, you're probably choosing some kind of pickup truck with 4-wheel drive and excellent towing capacity. Furthermore, you may prefer to purchase that 10-year-old Toyota instead of the brand-new BMW because the upkeep and maintenance costs are substantially lower. A tried and true platform like Toyota has a more robust and less-costly aftermarket for parts and service.

In the same way, Bitcoin miners choose their cooling type (and mining machines for that matter) based on their budgets, the technical requirements to successfully run machines, the availability of skilled labor to upkeep machines, and of course the efficiency of cooling and machine operation. It is incorrect to say that there is a single best method of cooling. Rather, it is more accurate to say that there is only a more optimal cooling method for the business model of the miner. The wisest of operators design their cooling systems and farms around their chosen business model and not uncontrolled variables such as predictions around the price of Bitcoin or network size and difficulty.

Mining Farm Footprint

Hand in hand with the discussion of cooling type is the exploration of mining farm scale and footprint. Bitcoin mining scales linearly in regards to electrical consumption and cooling requirements, i.e., one thousand Bitcoin miners require one thousand times as much electricity and one thousand times as much cooling as a single miner. While not immediately apparent, it should make intuitive sense that as one changes the amount of electricity one consumes in Bitcoin mining, you don't only need change the size and style of the cooling system, but also the physical structure of the building or container required to facilitate that cooling. While single-machine setups look radically different from 10,000-machine industrial mines, they all facilitate the same core functions.

Regardless of cooling type, every mining operation operates on two key design principles: it must protect the miner or miners from the environment and help regulate machine temperature via some controllable cooling or heating mechanism. Said another way, the Bitcoin mining farm, as a system, must be designed to allow the operator to have the greatest operational control and allow for the greatest machine longevity to suit their business purpose. Ramping up, ramping down, shutting off, or hashing through harsh environmental conditions all must be available to a miner looking to generate maximum revenue in their environment with their business model.

As a Bitcoin miner, and one who has likely invested a mean-ingful chunk of capital into hardware, it would behoove you to build some structure around your machines to keep them safe and happy as they incessantly munch on electrons. It would be unwise to purchase a Bitcoin miner and an extension cord, and proceed to put your brand-new machine on a card table in your backyard. While disapproving neighbors would be your first con-cern, rain, snow, dust, and the unrelenting summer sun will even-tually kill your miner. There *are* legendary mining machines, such as the Antminer S9, that are storied for suffering through some of the worst conditions (I've personally seen photos of astound-ingly dirty S9s that ran continuously in multi-story open-air farms in China, as well as S9s left on second story outdoor balconies during Wyoming blizzards to no ill effect). While operationally impressive, these machines are still computers, and computers are not known for their love of water or excess heat or cold.

Miners currently utilize four common footprints that employ environmental protection and temperature regulation design principles. Ordered approximately by scale of operation, they are home mining setups, modified buildings, containerized solu-tions, and purpose-built facilities.

Home mining arrangements are typically the smallest and most unique builds, consisting of custom enclosures, sound muf-fling, and often heat directed to various home processes such as HVAC systems or water heating. Modified buildings are gen-erally customized commercial spaces to hold tens, hundreds, or sometimes thousands of machines, and are often located in industrial areas for ample access to power. Containerized solutions can hold anywhere from dozens to many hundreds of machines, and are designed to be transportable and easily deployable in various environments and at various scales. The largest deployments of all are installed in custom-designed and purpose-built facilities, engineered from the ground up to optimize electrical capacity and machine operation in the tens of thousands of units and above.

Home Mining

The home miner is by nature a tinkerer. Their operation is generally limited by their home's electrical capacity and their spouse's patience for industrial-grade machines operating around their family. A typical residential electrical panel in the United States will allow for 100 to 400 amps of service.[68] Most of that electrical panel consists of breakers that protect and isolate various parts of your home and specific appliances. Running the current new generation of Bitcoin miners at home typically requires installing at minimum a standalone 20-amp breaker and a 240-volt electrical plug (the same as your electrical dryer or oven) for each machine.

If you're like me, and want to home mine and use your lights and refrigerator simultaneously, you are limited by the available breaker space on your electrical panel. You may not be able to operate a machine if you live in an old home or apartment that lacks appropriate infrastructure to home mine, or it may be three machines (or three 20-amp breakers, so 60 amps of dedicated service). Due to the constant load required by Bitcoin miners, expanding an operation at home becomes increasingly infeasible. Ten new generation machines would require at least 200 amps of space on an electrical panel, or the entirety of common home service here in the United States. What's more, as you attempt to scale at home, you find yourself mitigating two additional nuisances—excess noise and excess heat.

Most home mining setups consist of air or immersion-cooled systems and not hydro mining systems due to the additional infrastructure requirements and accessibility of retail scale suppliers. The simplest home mining setups consist of air-cooled miners in custom enclosures or small-scale outdoor containers, such as the Upstream Data Black Box. This product is an industrial-quality box with a hinged lid for machine access, and an internal design that protects the machines from weather ingress. Additionally, the box reduces machine noise while allowing appropriate operational airflow for machine cooling. For miners who want to mine inside of their homes using air cooling machines, other techniques and aftermarket products exist that allow for the use or evacuation of heat and the reduction of sound.

Some miners isolate their machines to basements or crawl spaces where noise is a non-issue and heat is often desirable. Others remove the stock fans from the machine and replace them with inline fans built specifically for HVAC purposes. This reduces noise and allows miners to conveniently direct exhaust heat for use in their home, using only off-the-shelf components found at most hardware stores.

Some miners modify how they operate their machine, reducing electrical draw, removing boards to drop electrical demand, and otherwise Frankenstein-ing together highly customized mining solutions that suit their home environment. Currently, there exists a set of easily accessible open-source and retail products that modify Bitcoin miners for use as home space heaters. The best known is the CryptoCloaks S9 Space Heater. This is a new and growing segment perfect for the home miner intent on learning how to operate an air-cooled machine and inclined to make use of a key mining waste product.

Oil immersion cooling, while rarer, is still accessible to the home miner. The more technically minded tinkerer will be able to assemble a system consisting of pumps, tanks, dielectric fluid, and a cooling radiator, though there is at least one commercially available solution from the company Fog Hashing. Their solution includes enclosures, radiators, all requisite tubing and connectors, and even dielectric fluid if requested. The costs of these systems will almost always exceed the costs of air-cooling setups. But the use of oil immersion in the home conveniently allows the use of excess heat for both air and water heating. That may be a hot tub or pool, hot water tank, or simply warming ambient air indoors from the radiator.

Home mining is an inherently creative domain and often the space from which the most experimental and innovative solutions emerge. Home miners, much like all hobbyists and tinkerers, aggregate in online forums and chat apps to compare systems and operational notes and oftentimes have some of the best machine performance in the industry.

Modified Buildings

Beyond the scale and quality of life limitations of home mining, the next scale of footprint for machine protection and temperature regulation is typically a modified commercial or industrial building. Deployments of this scale can range from tens to thousands of machines and are limited by the size of the electrical transformer they pull load from. As the name implies, a transformer transforms higher-voltage electricity from distribution

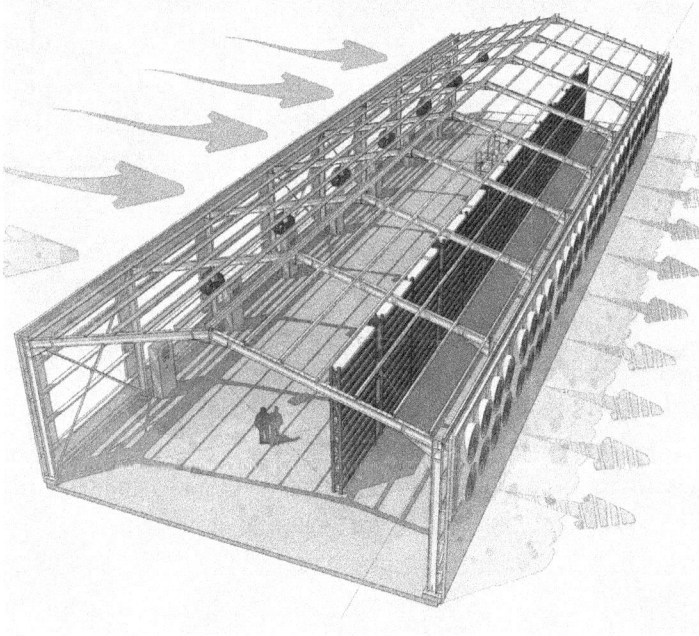

Figure 12: *A cutaway illustration of a modified industrial building for mining Bitcoin.*

lines that feed a region down to usable voltage for the mining machine. Transformers are limited by the amount of electrical load they can facilitate, ranging from thousands of watts up to millions of watts (megawatts). Depending on your transformer's size and performance rating, known as a K-Factor,69 most miners will estimate an approximate range of 240 to 300 new generation machines per megawatt of listed transformer capacity. Of course, as newer machines and cooling systems consume more or less electricity from the transformer, these numbers will vary widely.

The immediate draw of utilizing an existing structure as a Bitcoin mining farm is convenience of setup. For air-cooled facilities, racking, networking, and electrical components can be pieced together in-house or purchased from third-party vendors within and outside the Bitcoin mining industry. Most air-cooled systems in modified buildings use one of three arrangements: direct pass-through, shaped racking, or an in-and-up form factor. As each description implies, pass-through denotes air entering one side of a building and leaving from another. Shaped racking is the construction and ventilation of angled or multi-sided racking structures (like a three-sided box or V-angled racking within a building) that increases machine density within limited square footage. In-and-up arrangements that ventilate through the ceiling of the structure to allow hot air to rise and exhaust out.

All of these exhaust form factors may be deployed with only the powered fans onboard the machines to move air, or operators may add industrial fans to their buildings to increase the velocity and volume of air. Additionally, air-cooled miners will typically utilize some form of filtration to protect machines from dirt, dust, and inclement weather, and depending on geographic location may even integrate some form of hot air recirculation to protect miners during extreme cold.

Immersion and hydro mining are both accessible within modified commercial spaces. Due to their improved heat transfer coefficients, these systems consume more electricity in a smaller footprint when compared to their air-cooled counterparts. This provides benefits of space efficiency in building setup; however, as discussed previously, this comes with additional cost and complexity when compared to air cooling. A variety of vendors such as Hash House, Midas, Fog Hashing, and Heat Core build infrastructure to contain and cool both immersion and hydro machines using a mix of custom-built hardware and third-party systems.

These systems typically consist of some tank or miner racking system, pumping infrastructure to move immersion oil or water, and some form of radiator or dry cooler system to shed heat to the ambient environment. A suite of monitoring software keeps the entire operation under a watchful eye. When installing these systems, miners must account for placing their dry cooler or radiators outside the building instead of purely air-cooled systems. Instead of having to concern themselves with the characteristics of an airflow path through a building, they must plan to install all necessary piping to send and return water or immersion oil to an external dry cooler.

Containerized Solutions

Our third style of mining farm footprint may be contentiously referred to as the next largest in scale because containers typically range in size from twelve units to many hundreds, which is often smaller than a modified warehouse. While a modified

Figure 13: *An example of a containerized mining solution operating on an oil well.*

warehouse is limited by available infrastructure on site, containers may be deployed to the site of electrical generation as individual units or in large fleets. This characteristic of transportability, combined with their cost-effectiveness to produce—many mining containers are simply retrofitted shipping containers that can be purchased for a few thousand dollars and built in-house—make containerized solutions one of the most versatile methods of protecting and regulating machines at all scales. Containerized solutions are also operationally dependent on their available electricity, so transformer capacity plays a necessary role in operations.

The vast majority of mining container solutions are air-cooled systems. This is due both to the low cost to build and the speed at which these units can be built and deployed en masse. Holding to our two key design principles of environmental protection and temperature regulation, container designs fall into a few general shapes and formats that allow for control on both dimensions. The simplest designs cut opposing walls off of a container, using one as an air intake and the other as an exhaust. The intake generally utilizes some form of protective louvers or shielding to stop dust, debris, and weather from entering, followed by some form of air filtering (like an industrial version of the filter on your HVAC system you replace every six months). Once air moves into the container, it moves through the machines, accelerated by their onboard fans, and out through the opposite side of the unit. Often containers will use large industrial fans to increase the total volume of air, but some are still made as entirely passive units.

While the simplest air-cooled container units pass air through from one side to the other, there is some creativity in container air handling. Some units on the market put machines on raised racks down both walls of the container, intake air on both sides from the bottom half of the container, then exhaust it from both sides on the upper half. Other manufacturers produce versions where the container is raised a number of feet off of the ground, and air enters through the floor of the unit, then exhausts out through both sides of the container.

Additionally, containers may have air handling capabilities that allow them to either maximally exhaust air in summer conditions or recirculate hot air from the machine exhaust back toward the intake side during extremely cold conditions (container manufacturers have discovered that a "keep machines as cold as possible" strategy is not always optimal). In a hot and humid environment like the American South, maximum airflow is typically the most utilized operational setup. But in environments such as the American Midwest or Central Canada, where seasonal conditions vary widely, fine snow and extreme cold also pose an operational threat. When the intake of your machine is receiving extremely cold air (think sub-zero in Fahrenheit) and outputting air at 100+ degrees Fahrenheit, that difference in temperature across the machine hashboard causes damaging expansion and contraction. The ability to recirculate hot exhaust air back to the machine intake avoids thermal gradient issues.

Both immersion and hydro mining exist in the containerized solution space, and both have growing influence due to their improved machine cooling properties. The same elements of an immersion or hydro system in a warehouse, a machine container or racking, fluid, pumps, monitoring software, and a radiator or dry cooler, exist for containerized solutions. The difference is these systems are constrained by the small footprint of the container itself. These limitations have provided engineers with hours of what I assume is enjoyable tinkering. Much of the creativity comes from designing and making systems that can easily be transported and dropped on a mining site, which means designing for transport via an 18-wheeler. Additionally, there also exists a subset of options that contain both a mining setup and a genset, which consists of an engine and an electrical generator in a single unit. These deployments are typically small to mid-sized and are utilized to consume various excess, stranded, or waste gases from a producer.

Containers are some of the most creative and flexible setups for Bitcoin mining. Due to their cost, speed to build, scalability, and flexibility, they can be found anywhere energy exists. They also typify one of the greatest traits of Bitcoin mining, which is decentralization. Retrofitted or custom-manufactured containers for Bitcoin mining are essentially invisible to the lay-person, and allow miners to go to the market of energy instead of requiring that market to come to them.

Purpose-Built Facilities

The final boss for scale in Bitcoin mining is the purpose-built facility. Consuming tens to hundreds of megawatts of electricity on a single site and rivaling the consumption of tens of thousands of homes, these facilities and the businesses that build them require a skill set entirely different from the home miner, warehouse modifier, or container deployer. A smaller-scale miner may require a licensed electrician, city hall approval, or building inspection to build and operate their facility. Contrast this with a mega-mining facility, which will require extensive negotiations with a power provider for access to electricity, review under local, state, and federal regulatory agencies, and a small army of engineers, electricians, and mechanics to safely and efficiently conceive of and build the facility.

Mega-mining facilities must often construct their own substations, which draw power from high-voltage transmission lines through industrial-sized transformers and switchgear, to tens or hundreds of subsequent transformers arranged across tens or hundreds of acres of land. All of that electricity is eventually delivered to large, custom-engineered power distribution units and then to the individual machines themselves. Every megawatt of energy procured from a transmission line is eventually divided up into roughly 3,000 to 5,000-watt chunks that are consumed by each machine. By rough numbers, a facility of 100 megawatts can break down to anywhere from twenty to thirty thousand individual Bitcoin miners. Every watt of that energy must also be evacuated as heat to keep the individual machine from overheating.

In truth these facilities are in their infancy, with only a handful having been built since the birth of Bitcoin. Multi-hundred-million-dollar projects are implementing cooling strategies that are largely untried and untested by history. But while the engineering and operational challenges are immense, entrepreneurs are drawn by the strategic advantages that come from pure size, and are building modern marvels to air and liquid cooling in the name of mining Bitcoin.

Air and liquid immersion cooling are the two most common methods of mega-mining deployments. Similar to other scales of mining, air cooling is the most cost-effective method of building mega-facilities. While these custom-engineered buildings may stretch hundreds, and in some cases over a thousand feet in length, they utilize common building resources and practices in their components. They use many of the same cooling strategies

Figure 14: *An illustration of the inside of a purpose-built mega-mine.*

as containers or modified warehouses, such as large racking systems with a hot and cold side, intake filtration, and powered fans to increase air velocity. However, they do it at a scale that requires a dedicated full-time professional staff.

The same general rule applies to immersion cooling. While a mega-mining immersion building of 100 megawatts can live under the roof of a single structure, it will be cooled by smaller subsequent systems that include miner tanks, pumps, plate exchangers, and dry coolers or cooling towers. All of these systems exist to evacuate heat from the individual mining machine and eventually to the environment. Due to the infancy of hydro mining and the long lead times required to plan and build these facilities, hydro mining has not become a common choice for mega miners deploying capital and hash rate at scale.

Should you have the pleasure of exploring a mega-mining site someday, one of the most immediate things you will notice is that it feels much more like an industrial power plant than a high-tech supercomputing data center minting a new monetary asset. This may be surprising, but it should be obvious why. The single greatest input to Bitcoin mining at any scale is electricity, and at the largest scale, operators are dealing with electricity in inconceivable volumes. Every single ancillary system built into a mega mine, from the fans and filter walls to the adiabatic dry coolers serves the purpose of consuming and evacuating electricity in the final form of heat.

The Money Side of Bitcoin Mining

Just as a Bitcoin miner in your basement does not make a business, neither do 10,000 machines in a warehouse, yet the business of Bitcoin mining keeps machines humming along, day after day.

Every Bitcoin mining machine consists of the same four component parts, and requires the same three physical connections to operate, yet it is only in *how* the operator chooses to deploy their resources and control their inputs and outputs where they finally create the business.

A functioning business is an entity that produces a good or service at a profit. Your revenues minus your expenses must be a positive number to survive and grow. If that profit number is zero, you're alive. If it's negative, you won't be in business for long. Everyone from your local ice cream parlor to Exxon must follow this inviolable rule of business. While Bitcoin mining is a new industry, it doesn't obsolete the necessity to play by this rule. Your revenues must exceed your expenses.

It would be an impossible project to detail the various business models Bitcoin miners utilize to achieve the goal of profit. Rather, this section is devoted to breaking down the profit equation by exploring methods miners often use for revenue generation, and then follows by identifying the most common expenses they must control.

Generating Revenue

A Bitcoin miner primarily generates revenue from continuously contributing valuable hashes to a pool. That pool is rewarded for creating and adding valid blocks on the Bitcoin blockchain. Miners do not control the price of Bitcoin, the difficulty of the network (how many other miners are also searching to solve blocks), the amount of Bitcoin received in each block found, or the fees added to each block, yet each of these variables have radically changed the profitability of the mining industry by changing in value.

Should the price of Bitcoin, or the amount paid in fees, triple tomorrow, the monetary reward for mining Bitcoin will skyrocket and more miners will want to join the game of searching for valid blocks. Should the difficulty adjustment move upwards aggressively, due to increased competition, many miners will find themselves earning far less Bitcoin for the same amount of work as the hunt for blocks becomes a greater challenge. Should the price of Bitcoin plummet or fees dry up due to lack of network use, mining will become less rewarding and more competitive for those playing the game. Should the difficulty plummet, as it did after China banned Bitcoin mining and half of the miners went offline, many miners will be dusted off and plugged in previously unprofitable machines to take advantage of network conditions.

Fortunately, there is a single metric that captures these variables and aggregates them into a revenue value: hash price.[70] Coined by mining company Luxor, hash price allows a miner to easily calculate the expected USD value of their operation based on the hash rate they produce. Hashprice is commonly denoted as the value per terahash per day in USD (though it can be sliced and diced in shorter or longer durations and for larger units of hash power or any currency you like). For example, a miner with a single machine of 100T can calculate that at the hash price of $.0887/T/Day, they will generate $8.87 by running the machine at 100% power. Hashprice adjusts continuously as the variables within it vacillate up and down due to uncontrollable market conditions. That exact same machine, producing 100T over the last four years, at one time produced nearly $40 in a single day, as was the case in October 2021, and only a year later in October 2022 produced as little as $6.88 a day.

In addition to the variables that inform hash price, another metric consisting of controlled and uncontrolled elements informs mining revenue: hash rate capacity factor (HCF). The key difference between hash price and HCF is that while we do not control hash price, we *can* control elements of our HCF. HCF is typically denoted as a percentage, as is the case in electrical generators, and indicates to what extent we are performing work relative to our rated farm capacity. At 100%, we are using all of our machines at their rated terahash 100% percent of the time.

Unlike a large electrical generator, a Bitcoin mine can operate with a capacity factor below, at, or even in excess of its total nominal rating. For example, assume I have 50 machines rated at 100T. In total I have 5,000T of hash power—a nice-sized personal farm. Should excessive summer heat make running my machines at 100% power difficult, I may find myself underclocking my units to keep them from turning off due to excess heat, decreasing the total amount of power they draw and dropping the total terahash they produce. This will keep my operation from reaching a failure point during times of high heat, but it will negatively impact my total production of hash rate. My capacity factor will drop below 100% whenever I am executing this strategy, and the total amount of hash rate my farm produces will fall below 5,000T. But unlike electrical generators, I am also able to use advantageous conditions, such as cold weather or overpowered cooling systems, to overclock my machines and make them generate hash rate in excess of their rated terahash. This consumes even more power than a normal operating unit and pushes my capacity factor over 100%, allowing my farm of 50, 100T units to generate in excess of 5,000T of hash rate.

While it may seem appealing to advocate for maximizing hash rate capacity factor at all times, there are some details to consider. Remember our early introduction of the ASIC chip on the hashboard and our efficiency measure of joules per terahash. Recall that joules per terahash is the industry-standard method of measuring how efficiently a machine converts electricity into work (i.e., Terahash). The lower the number, the more proverbial "bang for your buck" the miner gets while operating their machine.

One consequence of ramping a machine down to produce less work and consume less electricity—or ramping a machine up to produce more work and consume more energy—is that the total J/T will become more or less efficient as a consequence. In the same way racing across town at 120 mph will get you there faster but will pummel your miles per gallon, or moseying along 10 mph under the speed limit may push your miles per gallon to the ceiling but delay your arrival, a Bitcoin mining machine varies in efficiency depending on *how* it is operated.

The four seasons are beyond our control, but we can supplement an overheating operation in midsummer with powered fans to reduce machine shutdown. We can't control a machine failing, but we can install better filtration in our facilities to reduce dust and debris, have a trained team to respond to problems, and ensure extra parts are in the supply closet when needed. These factors, as much as the day-to-day operating conditions of our farm, also impact our capacity factor and our ability to generate revenue by doing work with our Bitcoin mining machines.

If we get serious and write a formula to calculate our revenues, we could do so in the following format (Hash Price*Total Farm Hash Rate*HCF) = Total Revenue. By this formula, you might begin a granular exploration of the factors that influence revenues for your mining farm. If you're more of a Cro-Magnon operator like myself, you can just look at your pool earnings at the end of each month and be done with formulas and technicalities.

As an astute reader, you've noticed in answering the above question how a Bitcoin miner generates revenue, we stated they *primarily* generate revenue by producing hashes that have value. There is an entire set of additional sources of revenue generation that live entirely outside of the primary goal of running machines to generate hashes. In fact, they often live entirely outside of the Bitcoin network. These additional opportunities vary by size, location, and type of mining operation, but they provide real value to those they support.

For example, home miners and many small commercial operators mine Bitcoin not only for the rewards but also for heat. They capture and direct the continuous heat output by the machine into their living or working spaces as warmed air, through their hot water heaters for warm water, or even into their pools and hot tubs. In this case, Bitcoin mining not only generates revenue from hashes but uses the waste product of the mining process as a valuable input for another system entirely.

Other miners intentionally locate themselves near sources of waste or excess energy as discussed, and get paid to consume energy that would otherwise cost a producer resources to dispose of. That may be by mining in a remote oilfield near wells that are too far from a market or next door to a solar array to consume excess electricity during times of peak production when an operator has too much supply. Neither of these problems relate to the Bitcoin network and the production of hashes.

Rather, they are problems of the energy sector that are worth paying Bitcoin miners to help solve.

At the largest scale on the grid, mega miners can be called upon to ramp capacity up or down in response to the requests of grid operators. By ensuring hundreds of megawatts will either remain on or be available to turn off at a given moment, grids have a valuable resource for reducing price volatility and ensuring capacity during times of peak demand or limited supply. During those times, such as midsummer or during extreme cold events, mega miners will drop their electrical load on command, allowing generators more time to respond to consumer demand and adding greater price and supply predictability to an otherwise volatile market. These agreements, far outside the realm of generating hashes, provide immense value to a grid operator committed to providing stable and affordable energy for their customers.

With these cases in mind, we should update our above formula to now include other revenue sources, i.e., (Hashprice*Total Farm Hash rate*HCF) + Other Revenue Sources = Total Revenue. Stated more simply for us knuckle-draggers, total revenue is the amount of Bitcoin I earn over some period, plus everything else I save or am paid to do.

Operating Expenses

Revenue is only half of the profit equation; the other half is expense. Like other businesses, a miner incurs costs as either capital or operational expenses. Capital expenses include mining machines, buildings, containers, or other assorted infrastructure required to build and expand an operation. Operational expenses are your recurring charges, led by the cost of electricity, staffing, rent, consumable filters, dielectric fluid, or any and all other periodic charges that keep the lights on and the miners searching for blocks. The ways in which Bitcoin miners manage expenses are impossible to count, but two key principles of mining expenses hold true for operators. First, the largest outlay of capital at nearly every scale is for the mining machines, and second, the most critical operational expense for any mining site is electricity.

Bitcoin mining machines are expensive. It is not uncommon for the cost of machines to be multiples of the cost of a facility or containerized cooling setup. By rough example, one can often purchase a 1MW-sized air-cooled container for under $100,000. Within that container fits approximately 240 individual mining machines. As of winter 2024, the prices for machines vary based on performance and whether they are new or used and may be anywhere from $1,000 per machine for used units to $6,000+ per machine for state-of-the-art setups. This places the cost to fill your container at anywhere from $240,000 to $1.44 million dollars. Even more shocking, prices of machines react to the price of Bitcoin, often skyrocketing as the price runs up in parabolic advances. Machines that cost $1,000 today once fetched $12,000+ per machine at the peak of the last bull run. This same math plays out for immersion and hydro mining arrangements. While the multiple between machine and infrastructure is less dramatic due to the additional infrastructure costs, machines remain the largest capital expense for a mining operation.

The second principle of expenses is that electricity is the cornerstone operational expense. Should your cost of electricity be too high, you will find yourself producing Bitcoin at a cost above the current price of Bitcoin. This leaves an operator deciding to shut the operation off or risk running at a loss, hoping that an uncontrolled variable such as price, fees, or network difficulty improves financial conditions. The majority of operator effort goes towards reducing or eliminating the input cost of electricity by finding advantageous sources of energy, contractual advantages, or atypical uses for mining machines.

For example, large operators often purchase power under a contract called a Power Purchase Agreement (PPA). These contracts offer low electrical rates to large consumers with certain stipulations. These stipulations may include scheduled curtailment or the ability for a grid operator or generator to call upon the Bitcoin miner to shut down during certain periods of time. These agreements are beneficial to grid operators and generators because they ensure long-term demand and revenue for their operation while giving them the flexibility to allocate that demand elsewhere when needed.

Other miners choose to operate off-grid and source waste, excess, or stranded energy sources. This may take the form of a generator that has not yet connected to a grid but wants to generate revenues on site while they wait to interconnect, generators in remote locations operating at a fraction of their total capacity, oil and gas wells that are too far from a pipeline to be economically viable, or even landfills that produce energy in the form of methane and risk damaging the environment. In all of these cases, energy is a liability to the producer and a source of wasted revenues. This waste, however, is precisely what the Bitcoin miner seeks to keep their expenses below their revenues and continue operating profitably.

In addition to these exogenous factors, efficiency in the form of J/T emerges again as a key influence on our electrical expenses. An operation may have a nominal rating of 5,000T, as in our previous example, but it may be more cost-effective to operate it at a lower HCF to improve the efficiency of our electrical consumption. In the simplest terms, should I seek to manage my electrical costs as tightly as possible, I may choose to underclock my machines at 85T instead of 100T. This would be a 15% reduction in total hash rate produced relative to my total farm capacity. However, the consequence of this may be a 20% reduction in total energy used. In effect, the Bitcoin miner is pulling off of the accelerator slightly and slowing down to improve their fuel efficiency substantially.

PART TWO
THE BUSINESS OF BITCOIN MINING:
FOR EVERY MINER THERE'S A MODEL

Our **journey through** the *what* and *how* of Bitcoin mining started with the machine itself and the component parts. Understanding the four components of a Bitcoin miner gave us an assembled unit requiring three physical connections to operate. Moving outwards from the machine we explored those three connections, starting first with connectivity and the work of the Bitcoin miner through the ethernet cable. Through the electrical plug, we explored electricity and energy both on and off-grid, and how electricity makes its way from generation to the machine's power supply. We then stepped further up the supply chain, exploring the energy resources that feed generators and how energy is wasted. Finally, we looked at machine cooling and temperature regulation via air, immersion, and water, and how these various methods scale within various footprints.

Now we put the pieces in motion.

What follows are long-form interviews with Bitcoin miners of various scopes and scales. In their own words, miners of all types and scale, from the creative home miner prototyping custom peripherals to the CEO of a publicly traded mega-mining company, explain their philosophies, businesses, and visions for the industry.

While their machines all perform the exact same hash function and all consume electricity as a primary input, their businesses and goals could not be more varied. Some focus purely on the production of Bitcoin at the lowest cost possible, others utilize miner waste for personal or commercial use, and even others think of Bitcoin mining as a risk mitigation strategy for different industries entirely, caring little about hashes or the Bitcoin network.

As you explore their histories and the development of their businesses in the following pages, I hope you will see a nucleus begin to form, giving sense and order to an industry that appears chaotic at first blush. Armed with a core understanding of the machine, its inputs, and the industries that power those inputs, you should be prepared to apprehend what unites Bitcoin miners while appreciating what makes them different. By drawing these connections, you will understand the *how* of a Bitcoin miner, cracking open the door of *why* Bitcoin mining matters, and even catch a glimmer of where we are headed in the years to come.

Charlie Spears: From Oklahoma Oilfield Services to Mining on Natural Gas

The path of every entrepreneur is winding, and Charlie Spears is no different. Hailing from Oklahoma and raised in an oil and gas family, he has worked hard to align his passions with the family business. In the earliest days of Bitcoin, it was often assumed that mining only happened in large industrial warehouses or facilities located next to hydro operations in some distant Chinese

province. As the industry and technology matured and early oper-
ators refined their practices in the West, it became apparent that
mining could happen anywhere cheap energy existed.

This is where Charlie and his partners found their niche. They
paired their ability to operate Bitcoin mines with oil and gas well
owners looking to mitigate their waste products, and structured
unique deals that kept both parties happy. We discussed how he
learned the business of Bitcoin mining, how he sees the industry
maturing, and how some of the best mining operators sometimes
know very little about Bitcoin.

Who are you and how did you find yourself in Bitcoin mining?

I'm Charlie Spears. I live in Oklahoma. I've been in Bitcoin a very
long time. I won't say how long, but I'll put it this way: I thought I
understood Bitcoin, and then the Blocksize War happened. That
really dragged me down the Bitcoin mining rabbit hole. Prior
to that, I and the greater Spears family have been in oil and gas
for about half a century, with a small family office in oil and gas
consulting (specifically oil field services).

I thought I would never be able to work in or adjacent to
Bitcoin because all I know is oil and gas, but I found myself well
positioned to do this whole Bitcoin mining off natural gas thing.
Now it never followed a very straight line, but I managed to spend
way too much money on some Dragonmint T1s back in 2017,
plug those into a warehouse, buy more S9s at the bottom, then
find a lot of traction getting some partners together to build one
of the larger GPU mines in the country.

A few of us split off in 2019 to really lean into mining off natural gas and Bitcoin ASIC exclusive mining, and that brings us to

today. That partnership is called Nakamotor. We have a handful of sites off-grid here in Northeast Oklahoma. Those are mainly one or two container sites on small gas wells. Then we have a larger site, which is on-grid and about five megawatts. We are almost entirely self-funded and have been doing this for many years.

Do you remember the first machine you ran? Tell us about it.

Yeah, the Dragonmint T1. I didn't know anything about it. There were not a lot of agreed-upon metrics or even guides in English to explain how to hook up an ASIC or how to price these things. The idea of hash price and price per terahash were metrics not widely understood in the industry at the time. I was independent and didn't really know a lot of other Bitcoiners. I was still that crazy Bitcoin guy everyone knew. So I found my way into a Telegram group, sent a bunch of Bitcoin to somebody, and the machines showed up only a few months late. Then I realized that they ran on 240V power, so I had to get a couple of transformers step up and had to pay an electrician to rewire the panel at the warehouse. Then I just kept adding.

I didn't know what I was doing. I'm really glad the guy who owned the warehouse knew as little as I did, because both of us miscalculated the power rate. We agreed to sign a flat power rate and then about three months into it I was like, "Oh, I'm using twice as much power as I thought we would." We never really resolved it, but I did give him a nice bonus when I moved to the next place.

You know, there's a lot to be said for perseverance through unknown circumstances. I'm a strong believer that if you manage not to f*ck up too bad, and you hang on, you can at least enjoy the crazy margins which will follow at some point. I don't have that strategy anymore in my own partnership. We are more experienced and tactical about how we do things, but the price of Bitcoin going up can solve a lot of your problems.

My passion is Bitcoin mining off natural gas, which is really what I set out to do originally in 2017 and 2018. It took a really long time to get there. We didn't have any material operations until late 2020, and those did not go as planned. A lot of people think you can just walk up, like the classic Baby Boomer, just go in and shake their hand and ask for a job. This is not the case in oil and gas. In fact trying to crowbar the Bitcoin narrative into this world is probably going to work against you.

We learned through trial and error that we really have to put on the hard hat and really flex the oil and gas muscles, which my partners and I have. One's a reservoir engineer, one's the lead network engineer for one of the largest drilling contractors, and then my family has interests in oilfield services companies. So we know this business, and found we can use the tailwinds of the flare gas narrative to connect with people. But the real opportunity in our backyard in Oklahoma is in stranded and underpriced energy assets.

What is your business?

The American oil and gas industry is over 100 years old, and its primary goal has been to produce crude oil and or gas and deliver that to the market. We are introducing a new way to bring the market to the point of production. It changes how the deals are structured and how a lot of the infrastructure works.

Notice I didn't say Bitcoin anywhere alongside this. Bitcoin, as we all know, can consume energy anywhere in the world. Our business inverts traditional systems to figure out how to finance and technically execute. In oil and gas specifically, we've got all these wells around the country that produce oil and/or gas. It's very easy to find the natural gas, which is produced alongside the oil typically. The natural gas is hard to transport. That means in order for the gas to get to market, it incurs some cost, and sometimes that cost makes the real value of that gas at the point of production negative.

In situations like this, the gas is more of a liability to the producer and owner of the gas. Now it's never that simple in practice, because it costs a lot of money and is technically challenging to actually capture that energy in a way that makes sense. We found that if we take our little corner of Oklahoma, and we find a couple of producers of oil and gas, and we are able to find gas where it's either low or negatively priced for them, we can go and offer that producer a deal.

We can structure it in a few ways. The simple concept is that we bring a generator or generators to the site. We hook it up to their well (or string of wells) and we run those generators to a Bitcoin mine, which we put in a shipping container. That is the idea, and that's how we're able to achieve a very low cost of power. There's all sorts of trade-offs and conditions and challenges to do that, and even though it looks a little bit different than hooking up to the power grid, it's a really simple idea.

The power on a grid gets delivered to you on transmission lines and from substations. When you go off-grid on the wellsite, you produce the power on-site. You're basically the whole thing. You have to produce the energy, you have to generate the electricity, and you have to consume it. It means you have to wear a bunch of hats and it's very hard to scale. You can get a really low cost of energy, but at other risks such as uptime and capital expenditures.

What is your core thesis or strategy for Bitcoin mining?

You can have spot exposure to Bitcoin as an asset. You can own it. You can also have other exposure to Bitcoin in the form of equity of companies who build in the space. Bitcoin mining actually fits into this little niche, which I think works well as an infrastructure and energy play. You can have a cash-flowing asset within Bitcoin that allows you, if you are good at the energy side, to have Bitcoin exposure that produces cash. You can't get that with spot Bitcoin exposure. This helps justify the "Why do you mine Bitcoin over owning it?" question, because if you have a portfolio and you want to get exposure to Bitcoin, you have certain core competencies and strengths.

It checks all of these boxes in a portfolio. It's not like Bitcoin is this monolithic industry. It's diverse. You can know everything about Bitcoin mining and have no freaking clue how Bitcoin works under the hood. I find that we're now such a diverse industry that typically being an expert in one field means you have very little understanding of another. So when we look at a diverse exposure to Bitcoin, this is where Bitcoin mining really makes sense. I think some of the best Bitcoin miners actually describe what Bitcoin is quite incorrectly, but I don't think that matters much because they're very effective at getting hash online and keeping it there.

How do you manage your deals and sites?

We have to figure out three things before we feel confident in spending a lot of time and resources toward a deal. We need to make sure that the decision maker at the company wants to talk to us and is on board. We need to know pretty confidently how much that well or series of wells produces. We have to have some idea of the legality and royalties, because now we have gross production tax and royalty owners who have an interest in these wells, and it can get very complicated.

We do that due diligence and then we go back and forth for anywhere from 30 days to 2 years to hammer the details together. Then, Lord willing, we're able to marry that agreement with cash in hand to buy what we need. We may have to do some processing, some gas separation, or other things to the gas to make it run through a generator easily, then run that electricity to one or a series of containers that have the miners inside.

The generator is like a generator that sits outside of your house. We just take that generator and multiply it by 100 to 300. This is a common piece of equipment in the oil field. The oil field has a whole set of companies that provide services around the drilling and what's called well completion. There are companies that specialize in building and maintaining generators and deploying them around a region. We either rent or buy one of these generators. They come on trailers and you can roll them out to a site. It's a reciprocating engine typically.

It's going to be quite loud and it's going to be running constantly. I'll also emphasize that it's a bit different than the way these generators are typically run. These things are typically deployed to oil field sites for traditional oil field activity, to be run for a few days or as a conditional failover. But we use them as our primary power source, so we run them 24/7 ideally. It means we have to structure the contracts differently because the industry is not really designed to price these things to be run like we do.

Regarding containers, it's quite simple. You take a shipping container and you cut a hole in either side, you put a big shelf down the middle of it long ways, then you stack a bunch of these computers up. On one side is the intake and on the other side is the hot air blowing out. These computers are producing a lot of heat, they're consuming a lot of energy, and so if you walk around you'll have one side which has all these fans blowing out hot air, and on the other side you'll have what looks like to be little slits or hoods which have the intake for the air.

It's a very simple concept to grasp but very nuanced to optimize.

For the internet—this is the wild thing—the internet is probably the least important thing we need for mining. We just need to have a reliable connection to a cell tower nearby. We can run this off of a cell network, like a 4G cell signal. We get a big extendable antenna—these again are common in the oil field—and we just need to point that big antenna to a cell tower. That can connect a whole operation. Now there's obviously some asterisks and some conditions around that, but actually a very simple and inexpensive thing to do.

What is the future of your business?

One of the issues after you've been doing this a while, is you have to ask, "Do you really want to do it? Do you really want to try to scale?" In Bitcoin mining you're constantly trying to grow. You're almost always in a period of growth. We are evaluating how much the three of us really want to run it back again and try to build a mine that's ten times bigger, which requires a whole new skill set, capital formation, that kind of thing. We're happy with where we're at. We're positioned to mine Bitcoin going into the halving, then G-d willing a great bull cycle. We're at the place where our operations do not require constant maintenance and putting out fires.

The reality is the actual business of getting these things online and turning them online does require a lot of blood, sweat, and tears. We're cash flow positive, have always been, even when hash price was super down, but that came at great cost. The other side of the story is that it is extremely stressful to do all of this. I've been an entrepreneur in other categories and they pale in comparison to Bitcoin mining. For example, you don't have to justify the existence of running a retail store to your insurance provider. They're like, okay, we have a policy which is for your type of business, but in Bitcoin mining you have to explain what you're doing at a fundamental level, which typically spirals into philosophical conversations on the future of money and the world, and then you have to bring it back down to how does this particular insurance policy get rewritten for you? You have to be an expert on insurance to even get a policy.

What do most people misunderstand about Bitcoin mining?

There's a million ways to misunderstand it. I could be an expert in my particular type of Bitcoin mining and have very little insight into the business model of another miner. We may as well be different industries. We produce the same commodity, we use the same machines, but have entirely different business models. You see this in oil and gas, too.

In oil and gas you have tiny little operators who have family offices that have been going for 100 years and they own 40 wells out in the middle of Oklahoma versus the giant international, state-sponsored, super major oil companies. They may as well be totally different industries, but they produce the same commodity. In my view, this is a strength—the diversity of operators and strategies. This is one of the things I wish I could explain.

The other is how people always look at the price of Bitcoin today and your current economics and say, "How do you ever make money?" Technically Bitcoin does have to go to a high number in order for you to ever make money, and I say, "Yeah, I had this conversation in 2012, 2015, 2017, 2018, 2020, 2022, and I will have it for the rest of the decade, and I will always bet my money on Bitcoin being higher in the future."

You do have to assume that Bitcoin does go up on some timeline, and miners are putting their money where their mouth is. We are Bitcoin bulls, and we have a bunch of different ways of expressing how we think about that bullishness. It is the frontier, just like oil and gas has this wildcatter mentality of individual idealistic entrepreneurs, Bitcoin mining is very similar. We're going through a period of maturation as we figure out how to be grown-ups and not little cowboys in the industry.

Why does Bitcoin mining matter?

Bitcoin is a fascinating system that creates balance and security. Bitcoin mining and producing blocks hinges on proof-of-work and producing hashes with computers, which forms the vital backbone for the most neutral money. I'm more blockchain agnostic than a lot of people realize, but the only hill I die on is Bitcoin, because it is truly permissionless. I think proof-of-work underpins that permissionless nature of Bitcoin, and that's something worth a decade of my life.

What final thoughts are important to share or what have we missed?

My own little take on Bitcoin miners is that somebody can be really good at Bitcoin mining and not really understand other things about Bitcoin. If you are that person, recognize that, and if you are a person from the outside talking to a Bitcoin miner about Bitcoin, they may not have a very sophisticated understanding of an ETF. That's okay and does not invalidate them from being able to be a really effective Bitcoin miner. We're now in this very diverse industry where you can try to be a jack of all trades, but really Bitcoin is going to bend towards the masters of little sectors.

Kent Halliburton: Zero Emission Hosting and Bitcoin Acquisition as Intended

As an early-stage industry, Bitcoin mining borrows strategies from the technological innovations that preceded it. One such case is rooftop solar, where Kent Halliburton, CEO of Sazmining, cut his operational and sales teeth. After nearly a decade and professional success in the booming industry, Kent found himself overseas, in love, and obsessed with Bitcoin.

In hindsight, leading a hosting company that runs entirely on carbon-free energy sources seems a natural fit. Kent's vision for the business is Bitcoin acquisition as it was originally intended, and his focus is on aligning customer and business incentives. He borrows and expands upon the lessons he learned helping homeowners add decentralized energy production to their property with solar arrays. Sazmining is differentiating itself among a glut of startup hosting operations and working to establish a reputational moat that will allow them to accelerate adoption via Bitcoin mining.

Who are you and how did you find yourself in Bitcoin mining?

I'm Kent Halliburton, CEO and co-founder at Sazmining. I worked the first half of my career from 2005 to 2014 in rooftop solar. At the top of my game there, I was running a sales organization to build out rooftop solar projects, customize software coordinating operations, and lead mergers and acquisitions. I was responsible for nine-figure sales targets and had a team of 100 staff. It was a lot. It was a publicly traded company, and the board in all of their wisdom brought in a new CEO, and I decided that this was the right time for me to hit the exit after I saw where the CEO was planning to take things.

I always had a dream of seeing the world. I had a flush bank account and took a couple of years, grabbed a backpack, traveled around the US, South America, and Europe, and along the way fell in love with a Portuguese woman. This was circa 2015, the same year I discovered Bitcoin. I got my grubby little paws on a couple of Bitcoins towards the end of that year. I wish I had done a whole lot more, as all of us do, but I found myself utterly fascinated with it. By the time I planted a flag in Portugal at the beginning of 2016, I realized that I wanted to build the next leg of my career in this space.

I tried my hand at a couple of entrepreneurial efforts in Portugal, but it was completely new. I was on foreign ground, didn't know the language very well, didn't have much of a network, and there was a lot of red tape. You know, Portugal is not the US, and I struggled quite a bit. I tried all sorts of different ways to acquire Bitcoin; I did some consultancy services, tried mining at home, tried trading, got sucked into the sh*tcoin wheel of Samsara, which all of us have to go through at some point.

By the time 2018 came around, I knew that I wanted to focus strictly on Bitcoin. I heard Will, the founder of Sazmining, speaking on a solar podcast. I knew the host, and they agreed to put us in touch. I got to know Will a little bit and said, "Hey, do you need some help?" Will said yes, and I came on as an energy advisor, then along the way helped to raise some capital, developed a couple of projects, and now am the CEO of Sazmining.

Do you remember the first machine you ran? Tell us about it.

I got suckered into an advertising scheme. This was back before I purged myself of crypto scamming completely. There was a company called, I think, OneMine. They sold this box that I purchased and plugged into the wall, and Ethereum, Monero, and Bitcoin were the three coins that I could mine. I was excited about the bull market gains and I was like, "This seems cool, it seems easy."

I plugged it in and soon discovered it was a total scam from my vantage point. They've closed up shop since. It would sit there and whirl, and I'm convinced that somebody somewhere had some miners behind it. In the interface I'd be deposited different amounts of Bitcoin that never seemed to correlate to the actual network. I was like, "This is ridiculous." I got my money out of it, but just. The core driver for it was the fact that I wanted to be able to mine from home and do it in an easy way, so I do think that experience ultimately did shape the product that we are creating at Sazmining. When I was doing Bitcoin consulting and helping people with the IT side of Bitcoin, I would constantly get through to completely brand-new people, and as soon as they would hear about Bitcoin mining it was, "Oh, can I go mine my own?"

I think that there is a latent desire when people hear about Bitcoin to actually be able to access mining. Really, that's the native way to acquire your Bitcoin, as Satoshi designed it. As opposed to being on an exchange and going through all of the KYC and the rigamarole, there's no temptation for me to sell, because I know that I need to have an ROI with my mining rig to be able to make the investment make sense. So I'm just acquiring my Bitcoin, and I'm literally not thinking about it. It's even easier than a DCA. It's a single one-time purchase and I have my monthly electricity bill paid for on my credit card. My Bitcoin just continues to accrue in my wallet. I don't think about it. That was not the same for selling goods or services and that was not the same for trading.

What is your business?

Our business is to obsolete the exchanges. That's what our business is, and I know that sounds radical and hard to perceive. When we crafted our business, it was not clear at that time. In an early-stage startup, I feel like you have an idea, but you have to continue to walk down the trail and leave that idea in your back pocket to bounce around with a bunch of other thoughts. Eventually it polishes itself smooth, and you can see it. That's what happened with us.

If you think about Bitcoin's adoption, I would argue that regardless of what you think of Coinbase, in 2012 when they opened their doors, they were the first organization to actually make Bitcoin accessible through an exchange-based experience. Adoption skyrocketed. There was a measurable increase. That's where I went for my first Bitcoin in late 2015, and it was a great experience. I think things have changed since. I no longer utilize Coinbase, but when Will and I set off building this company, we realized that Coinbase made adoption easy because of access. But if we look at how the distribution of Bitcoin was designed originally, that access was through mining, and nobody has made that easy.

So first we went out and hired an elite design firm. We wanted to test and validate that our designs hit the mark on the user experience side. By the time we built our product, we realized we had a better way to acquire Bitcoin—not only better in terms of the user experience, but also in terms of the feel. We had tied ourselves to clean energy for all our mining operations, so despite all the Bitcoin energy FUD, people felt like they had the moral high road when they were using our product.

A lot of people are also just scared of the exchange experience. I think the exchange experience is actually limiting Bitcoin adoption right now. It's not a natural experience for a person to have to wire money to an exchange, then go to that exchange and look at this jagged line and say, "I want to buy now." It is actually a much more comfortable experience for a client to make a couple of clicks, buy a device, and have a steady stream of sats coming to them. We wind up removing all of the price volatility, removing the KYC-related risks, removing exchange blowup risk from a counterparty. It's frankly the best way to acquire sats.

There are hard costs to mine though, and there's no way around them. That is where the proof-of-work comes in and the rubber meets the road. But those hard costs have to be borne by somebody, and we as a service provider have to make money to provide our service. We had a good hard think about where we are going to extract profit in this business model to perform our service. We decided pretty early on that the more that we align incentives with our clients, the more that we are going to behave in the way that clients would want us to behave.

That means we do revenue sharing. We said, let us tie our fate to the same fate as a client, and let us find a mining pool that will allow us to split the reward when it's paid out, so we never custody or touch the Bitcoin. That's just 15% of the rewards now, and what that means is not only are our margins totally transparent, but it also allows us to conclusively tell our clients we care about how quickly their mining machine is turned on, we care about how quickly we turn around repairs, and most importantly, the number one factor we care about is uptime. If you're not up and generating hash, we're not either, so we have 100% aligned interest with our clients.

To be concrete, how do you manage your electricity and temperature on sites?

We are running a capital light model, which means that we have a pretty extensive and exhaustive process to decide who we're going to partner with at any location. We're only in two locations right now, Wisconsin and Paraguay, and after Paraguay we should be positioned to go after a big enough chunk of power that we can possibly even partner up with one of the publicly traded companies, because we offer a unique value proposition. We can cycle capital to them from a market that they don't have access to.

As far as the operations on the ground are concerned, in this case in Paraguay, what we're using for cooling is a water curtain in a modified warehouse. Machines are in the middle, and on the opposite side are massive industrial fans that suck air, and pull it across and through the machines. In Paraguay, we don't really have any heating needs. The lowest temperatures are mid-60s, and in the summer it is much hotter.

We have been facing curtailment in the summer months. Even though it's hydroelectric, there's only so much local grid capacity for power, and the utility can only push so much electricity through so big of a pipe, regardless of how much power is available on the high-tension level. That means that there are upgrades going on locally for substations to bring down that high voltage and make more capacity at a consumer level. We've actually integrated ourselves as a dispatchable load directly with the utility office. The benefit of that is it helps the utility to be more granular in production and transmission, and it helps us to receive more power overall.

And what about connectivity?

We have redundant internet connections and never have data transmission issues. I think most Westerners would be surprised at the level of connectivity that's available throughout Latin America. I only see it getting better, especially with Starlink. If you come to a place, like where I am in the Amazon, it's just a night and day difference from the local internet. The internet's not horrible, but it's a bit bouncy. Everybody jumps online in the middle of the day and suddenly I can't have video calls. Throw up a Starlink antenna, and it doesn't matter where I am in the backcountry. As that technology is being deployed, if I have a service plan with Starlink, I'm no longer lost anywhere in the woods. I'm always connected, and the implications are wild to think through.

What is the future of your business?

The future of the business is winning the reputation game. That is everything for this business model. There's been an overwhelming amount of demand because it's cheaper to mine Bitcoin than it is to buy, so people are always going to be throwing money at this business model. However, there's been an underwhelming amount of quality supply to meet that demand. That's been the problem. All we have to do is show up and meet that demand in an honest way, with integrity, and the world's our oyster.

I've built my career based on retail-based operations, so I see it as a huge opportunity, and what I think a lot of folks miss about that opportunity is by winning a reputation game, you effectively own the customer at the top of the funnel. What it does is give us the latitude to add value-added services that make our business more profitable. The client then has a better experience.

Some of those might be insurance-based products, performance guarantees, or financing solutions. There are other potential side services. Perhaps storage solutions for the Bitcoin miner, tax-based services—there's all sorts of different ways this can go. What we imagine is an ecosystem that surrounds and contains the customer experience such that clients prefer it to going to an exchange to acquire their Bitcoin. It's safer, more secure, and easier.

What do most people misunderstand about Bitcoin mining?

Proof-of-work. I think they're so mystified by the idea of proof-of-work that they can't evaluate the business case for it. I understand that mystification, and I think it's incumbent on us as an industry to try to educate. The best metaphor I've heard came from Braiins—this idea of a thousand people sitting down and rolling dice. We need some way to make the concept of proof-of-work accessible for people to move past this just being an imaginary way to generate Bitcoin. Gold mining was pretty understandable, right? I go in with a pick and ax and I dig in the dirt. I find a chunk of gold, and it's mine. If people don't understand the *how* of Bitcoin mining, it's hard for them to deploy capital into it.

What final thoughts are important to share, or what have we missed?

This is a unique perspective that I have from living through the rooftop solar industry. In the 2005 to 2010 era, I was watching the technicians and experts use their jargon to sell rooftop solar. I watched them get washed out of the industry. They got washed out because they didn't upgrade their language to meet clients where they were at. It's my perception that we're seeing something similar occur with mining right now. Although the technicians and all of their jargon is 100% accurate, the language set we use needs to change. I think it's incumbent on us to drive that change sooner than later because as we make this industry more accessible, more capital flows into it, making the network more secure, and leading to greater adoption.

Bob Burnett: From the Corporate C Suite to a Leader in Decentralized Mining

The hallmark of a successful entrepreneur is the ability to see around corners, to predict trends, and to be in the right place at the right time when opportunity emerges. Most of all, a successful entrepreneur comes to the starting line of their business with some wisdom already in hand. This is the story of Bob Burnett. Having spent decades helping to bring the emerging home computing revolution into being, Bob started his career as a young engineer in the emerging field of laptop computing and grew into the CTO role at a multi-billion dollar corporation.

That wisdom, gained along the way, gave him the foresight to develop a unique but powerful strategy in the world of Bitcoin mining. Choosing to remain private at the expense of massive public investments, choosing to deploy small and mid-scale operations instead of deca- or centi-megawatt facilities, and embodying the core Bitcoin thesis of self-sovereignty at every level has served Bob in growing Barefoot Mining and establishing him at the head of the pack in decentralized mining operations.

Who are you and how did you find yourself in Bitcoin mining?

I'm Bob Burnett. I am the CEO and founder of Barefoot Mining. I entered Bitcoin, I like to say, through the back door. My history is that I came from the personal computer industry, going way back to the mid-80s. My first job out of school, with a degree in computer engineering, was with a company called Zenith, which used to be a major TV brand. They also had a personal computer division during the infancy of the personal computer market. By sheer luck, I was a very junior member of a team that was developing what I believe to be the world's first laptop. I ended up with that as my catalyst, spending the next 20 years in the personal computer industry, eventually as the Chief Technical Officer of Gateway. I was part of the team that took them public in the early '90s. We reached about $10 billion in annual sales, we had 25,000 employees, so we were a big company globally.

By 2017 I had left Gateway and received a phone call from a former Gateway acquaintance, and he said, "Bob, I need several hundred Ethereum mining servers. Can you get a bunch of Nvidia chips, and can you design them for me?" Gateway was the first company to design Nvidia silicon into a computer, so when they were a startup, Gateway was the first company to give them a chance. So I (together with Keith Thomas, the now-president at Barefoot Mining) reached out to Nvidia. They remembered us and said, "We'd be happy to give you some chips. We trust you." We ended up taking this deal and forming Barefoot Mining as a company, initially to design Ethereum servers. After fulfilling that deal, we said, "Well hey, we have this design, does anybody else want to buy them?" Surprisingly, a lot of people did—at least surprising to us.

We were thinking about it as computer people, but of the people saying they wanted to buy them, almost all said, "I'll buy some, but only if you'll host them for us." So as an enabler to sell more Ethereum mining equipment, we started hosting. About a year in, we started to look more seriously at what Ethereum really was, because again, we were wearing this computer hat. We weren't thinking about it as a new economic tool, a new monetary system, none of those sorts of things. I started looking especially deep at what Ethereum was, and what they were trying to pull off technically. I thought it was getting too complicated. By then, they had announced the shift from proof-of-work to proof of stake (although they hadn't done it yet). I didn't like it.

I have a background in economics in addition to my technical degree. I'd been into Austrian economics since the early 2000s. I said, "Well geez, I don't like the monetary policy." So I looked more deeply at Bitcoin. I fell in love with it. We pivoted as a company to Bitcoin. We wanted to design our own equipment. We didn't have the money to design our own ASIC (by that I mean the chip), so we did the next best thing. We signed a deal with Bitfury to become the US distributor for their equipment. We did that in 2018, and then we started building out Bitcoin mining operations, and here we are today.

Do you remember the first machine you ran? Tell us about it.

The Bitfury systems are somewhat unique and I fell in love with them from the computer design aspect. Today I still say they are the best from a system perspective, the best-designed equipment the market's ever seen. They're built more like a traditional server, so they're built as a 19-inch rack-mountable 6u chassis. They fit in more of a traditional data center application. They consume 6,300 watts, so very high power consumption. The design is like opening a computer chassis. It's very easy to get inside. It has what's called a black plane design, meaning there are eight hash boards that go in a typical unit, so it was very familiar to us. They run on 277 volts, so there are a lot of great things that come from that.

We were very, very impressed by them. They were frankly designed in the way that I, as a computer designer, would have likely designed the unit. It was funny for us, because it was only after our initial experience with the Bitfury equipment that we started working with the Bitmain equipment, and the Whatsminer equipment, and some of the other ones. We were very disillusioned by what we perceived to be the lack of quality and design of those units. We're forced to use them today, but they're not very good, frankly. Bitcoin mining is dragging behind the personal computer market in the same way personal computers followed servers in the seventies. It's a decade or so behind those platforms. It's a natural course of things, and we need more competition.

What is your business?

I looked at the Bitcoin mining landscape, and to me it was clear that there were three classes of miners and specific mining sites. I'll talk about it at the site level, but it extends to the company. I categorize them in three buckets. One is the elephants: these are sites, typically tens of megawatts or more, certainly going into the hundreds of megawatts. They're big and powerful sites, but they're slow to bring up. They typically take a year to a year and a half to put together. They're slow to grow, just like an elephant. You know, the gestation period of an elephant is really long, but ultimately they're big and powerful. They're also basically stationary, which makes them easy to hunt. So that's the elephants.

The other end of the spectrum is of course the rabbits. The rabbits are the individual miners, an S19 in the garage, maybe it's a small business that throws an extra S19 in a server closet. Individually, they're not very powerful. Collectively, they can be massively powerful, just like overbreeding rabbits can ruin a farmer's field. And if the farmer goes out to start to hunt them, he can certainly shoot a couple of rabbits, but the act of shooting a couple of rabbits scatters them. He'll never catch them all. Compare that to the elephants. By definition it's almost impossible for there to be too many elephants, and they're stationary. So if you go to start hunting elephants, if your mission was to kill all the elephants, you probably could.

Then there are the horses. The horses are in the middle. The horses are small to medium-sized commercial sites. This might be several hundred kilowatts to let's say single digit megawatts. You can build them relatively quickly. They can go from conception to being functional very quickly. We've done them as fast as five or six weeks, to go from "Hey, we found an opportunity, let's go implement it," to running five weeks later. We're dealing with less regulatory compliance, more off-the-shelf components. If we need a one-megawatt transformer, easy to get. We need a small disconnect; we need 300 servers. All these sorts of things can come together very quickly, so you can get up and get going. Horses are typically built in a mobile fashion. They're usually in hash huts or containers, so if you start shooting horses, the horses can scatter very quickly.

If you said, "Bob, you can have one 100-megawatt site, or you can have fifty 2 megawatt sites," what I decided was I would choose fifty 2 megawatt sites. I think I'm probably different from a lot of people in that way. They would think, "Why would you do that? Wouldn't it be more operationally efficient to be all in one place?" There's some truth to that. There are probably more resources. But here's the thing: if we had two groups, one group is going to build one 100-megawatt site, and another group's going to build fifty 2-megawatt sites, I can start building 2-megawatt sites, and I can be operating and generating Bitcoin *way* before any of the 100-megawatts comes online.

I'm just throwing a number out, but let's say I build in the space of the year it took to bring a 100-megawatt site up, I might be able to get 12 or 15 of these other ones up. So we're generating hashes earlier. I'm going to raise the money as the sites become more possible, so I'm going to deploy the capital very close to when the sites come up. If market conditions change dramatically, I can stop. I also haven't put all of my eggs in one basket, so if something happens like taxation, regulation, or community resistance, I'm very diverse. I have different power sources. I'm in different jurisdictions. I've got all of these different variables. I understand there's pros and cons of each type of site, but we have chosen to be the horse-class company. That's what we want to do.

How do you manage your electricity, connectivity, and heat?

I'll answer the question in a bit of a different way. I wrote an article a while ago on something called the miner trilemma. Whenever a site needs to come together, three things have to come together: energy, the mining equipment, and money. My theory is that, if you want to get started on a project, at any one point in time, one of them will always be hard. We've just lived through the last year and a half of this bear market, and in that bear market, from my perspective, mining equipment has been easy to source and at a good value. So you could get servers at a good value, and you could get them quickly, especially in the volumes for a horse-class site.

The venture capitalists, the angel investors, the high net worth individuals, who I normally access to bring up sites, there's been a lot of reluctance. If we back up before the last bear market, during the last bull run, energy was not super hard to get, and it was easy to get the money, but getting the equipment was difficult, and it was overpriced. In the trilemma, we went from the post-China mining ban boom period, where cash was easy and equipment was hard, and then they flipped positions. I think now we sit here in early 2024 probably getting ready for another pivot.

So when I'm putting up a site, the question is, do I even do a site? Can I make these three things come together? I think to be a long-term successful miner, as the difficulty shifts in the trilemma between these three vectors, you have to have the skill sets to navigate. I think a lot of companies come up when they have a competitive advantage in one of the three vectors, and they find some success. But when the market shifts, if they haven't acquired the skills to be successful, they're going to fail.

Now in terms of operations, at present we have found that air-cooled solutions provide us with better economic return. We're certainly intrigued by immersion and hydro, but right now we find that we can get a better economic return from air-cooled. We still have one fixed facility, one old data center that we converted, but we've gone 100% to containers or hash hut type solutions. In part that's because we found there are some great vendors out there: Upstream Data, Digital Shovel, and Cipher. There's other good ones like Giga. There are plenty of good providers of these containers, and they have largely solved the problems of cooling. Even in South Dakota—the majority of our operations are in South Dakota—we have very few issues with air cooling. We are located in areas where energy is almost never at a deficit relative to what the community needs, so we're never turning off. We prefer that. We're in the business of mining and not playing the energy game. We want to run 24 by seven and just go.

You asked about connectivity. I'll say this: we really value sovereignty. I've been public about this. One of our projects is a hydroelectric facility in South Carolina. A few years ago we acquired the rights to an old textile mill with a hydroelectric system that was in disrepair. We raised money, we rehabilitated that infrastructure, and we mine off-grid using that energy. We had the option of connecting back in and selling energy surplus to the grid, but we cut that cord. We did it knowing that from a purely economic perspective, it might cost us money at a few periods during the year, or rather it was an opportunity cost. But what it did was free us from a bunch of regulatory oversight, and maybe somebody demanding that we route our energy out there. If it's not physically possible, then we don't have to worry about it. It's different philosophically from the way a lot of companies operate, but we really value sovereignty and our long-term ability to control our own destiny.

What is the future of your business?

First of all, I want to spread my footprint. I want to get outside of the US. I think that's very important both for me and for the network. If we look at the horse size class, let's say a few hundred kilowatts to several megawatts (but single digit), whether it's on-grid or off-grid, there's almost an infinite number of them. I think one of the things that's harder if you're an elephant is you either have to develop these massive sites, including sub-station buildouts, or you have to find energy which is underutilized, which I think is going to get harder and harder with time.

Here's a brief example using one of our sites. It's a place in South Dakota; we found an industrial park. We were aware of a business that had been consuming a decent amount of energy that had left. A new business went into this site that wasn't using as much energy. They make burritos in this factory. We knew there was a little over 2 megawatts available. So we approached the landlord. We said, "Can we throw some containers on the back side of your building? No one will even notice that they're there, and we'll pay you rent to use the land, and have access to the power."

The electrical company was very happy; the usage model went back up, and we've got a couple of megawatts in that spot mining in the back parking lot of a burrito factory. Nobody even knows we're there. I think that opportunity exists all over the world, where a substation is slightly underutilized, you can come in and provide base load. I'm pretty sure I could spend the rest of my life just developing those little sites, and by the way, there's not much in maintaining a site like that. It's a part of a person, and it's not hard to find somebody technically competent enough to handle the day-to-day management.

What do most people misunderstand about Bitcoin mining?

Bitcoin mining is a lot more than hashing. If someone wants to just be a hasher, that's fine. It's certainly their choice to be a hasher. But Bitcoin as an ecosystem needs a lot of miners. We're sitting at a point where mining is really done by the pools, and there's only a couple of pools in the world. Ninety percent of all the hash rate is with six pools. Those six pools create all of the block templates, which for those less technically knowledgeable means that they are the ones selecting the transactions that go in blocks. To me, that's too easy of an attack vector. Four of those pools are Chinese-based, two of them are US-based. Nothing against any of those pools individually, but collectively I think they have too much power. If we want to have a censorship-free ecosystem, then we have to have a substantial number of miners become block template creators. This is a critical juncture where we can really decentralize this thing or we can massively centralize it.

What final thoughts are important to share, or what have we missed?

The mining community has, in my opinion, largely lost its vision. It's difficult to find many mining companies that are actually mining companies. Most of them are capitalistic hashers. There's a big distinction, and I believe it presents some existential risks to Bitcoin as we know it. For instance: I think miners no longer consider things like block template creation as part of their purview. They have let the pools take that role on. While the economic incentives in the short term don't change much, in fact I can do less work for the same or more money means the control point changes.

It takes them out of the decision process about what transactions to include, and some of the power that I believe will come in the long run. Fork activations mainly come through that power, so you're losing your ability to participate in those things–the next

Segwit, the next Taproot, should CTV be activated? Miners lose their power base. Also, some of the big guys can't hop from pool to pool without some gymnastics. When you're a public company, you have auditors, CFOs, and the SEC. They have oversight over what pool you use. You can't just change it. Technically to change to a new pool is trivial, but as a practical matter, it will take you months to change a pool, to get all of the approvals and everything in place.

Econoalchemist: Privately Mining Bitcoin at Home

Somewhere in the intermountain West lives privacy advocate and educator Econoalchemist. His research and guides on varied topics, from seed phrase storage to sound-dampening systems, have become ubiquitous for individuals looking to take both their personal and Bitcoin privacy more seriously. We connect with Econoalchemist to explore his history in Bitcoin mining, how and why he built his home mining system, and what he learned along the way in this nascent corner of the Bitcoin mining world.

His reasons for home mining have always aligned with his personal dedication to individual privacy. Because of this, his work in the 'business' of Bitcoin mining, if he would even call it that, has always been driven by both monetary and ideological factors. This makes home miners like Econoalchemist a powerful force for innovation. They are willing to create new methods and test innovations in ways a more purely profit-driven entity may not be able to.

Who are you and how did you find yourself in Bitcoin mining?

I go by the pseudonym Econoalchemist. You may know me from various guides I've written on how to use Bitcoin in a manner that preserves self-custody, censorship resistance, and privacy. That's how I fell into the Bitcoin mining rabbit hole. I was really looking for a way to accumulate more Bitcoin without attaching my identity to those Bitcoin transactions. For example, most people use KYC exchanges [Know Your Customer], and that information is collected by the exchange, various three-letter agencies, and governments that have access to that information. Hackers have been able to get that information and dump it on the dark web, and it can be collected and used against you by aggressive tax authorities who want to collect unrealized gains or wealth taxes.

I was trying to figure out a way that I could get more Bitcoin without having to use anything associated with my identity. Around the time that I was trying to figure out this puzzle, I read a guide by @Diverter_NoKYC called "Mining for the Streets." That's when the light bulb really clicked for me. I could just buy this computer, plug it in, and get Bitcoin by paying my utility provider for the electricity I used. No one would have to be any wiser about the Bitcoin I was receiving on the back end of that transaction.

Up until that point, before Diverter published his guide, you would be hard-pressed to find anyone out there telling you that mining Bitcoin at home was a good idea, let alone giving you detailed step-by-step guidance on how to do it. The narrative at the time was that you should not mine Bitcoin at home, that only industrialized players can mine it, and that you were wasting your money. So I put out my own guide and confirmed what Diverter was saying.

Do you remember the first machine you ever ran? Tell us about it.

I still have it. It's sitting next to me. I have a little DIY Black Box underneath my workbench. In it is the very first miner I bought.

It's a Whatsminer M31s, an 82 terahash model. I bought it from the guys at Blockware. I reached out and Diverter said, "You want to use these specific Telegram groups, you want to avoid using eBay," so on these Telegram groups I searched and I saw an ad from Blockware Solutions for this miner, and they wanted, I think, $2,800 for it at the time, which was a lot of money to me.

I was like, gosh you know I could just buy Bitcoin with this, but I want to do something that enables me to accumulate more Bitcoin than just the Bitcoin I could buy with the money. I was already sold by that point. I contacted Mason at Blockware, and I remember haggling with them on the price, which is just ridiculous in hindsight, because within a year that same miner quadrupled in value. It was worth almost $10,000 at one point, and I remember trying to haggle him for something like 50 bucks here and there to get the price down as much as I could.

I took a leap of faith and sent them the money, and they sent me the miner. It showed up in the mail, and I just remember that it was a whole new frontier. I had done multiple guides at that point, but those were on hardware wallets or steel plates, but having this industrially rated machine that could produce Bitcoin that's built to go into a factory—and I had it sitting in my living room at home. I felt like it was such a new frontier, like stepping into this totally uncharted territory that I wasn't sure where it was going to take me.

Then it was what do I do about powering this thing? All of the details started in the back of my head. I had to figure out how to get electricity to it, how to get ethernet to it. What was I going to do with all of the hot air that was coming out of it?

I knew it was going to be hot and loud, but I didn't really know how loud or how hot until I actually plugged it in and ran it for the first time. It was a lot more than I expected. I realized very quickly why this machine belongs in a warehouse and not in a residence. I did the best I could to come up with a way to mitigate the sound. I built a little wooden box. I've got a background that involves sound, so I tried to incorporate some lessons I had learned from designing recording studio spaces.

What is your business?

The business is paying my utility provider for electricity and getting Bitcoin on the backside of that transaction. That's a great business when hash rate is low, when the price of Bitcoin is high, when you have cheap electricity, and when the efficiency of the miner isn't particularly important. It's a terrible business to be in when any of those variables change.

As we've seen, hash rate has gone through the roof and the price has bombed. It turns out my electricity rates are a lot higher than I thought they were, and from a strictly business perspective, if we want to look at it through that lens, I would say that personally I failed the test pretty miserably. If I had been running a business, I think that business would have failed in the long run.

Now fortunately there's utility in mining and accumulating Bitcoin that's not tied to your identity. It isn't strictly a business for my objectives, so I have freedom there that I don't really have to treat this hobby like I would a serious business. My objective is just to accumulate Bitcoin, and because of the utility in the heat that the ASIC produces, even though the Bitcoin price is low, even though my electricity rate is high, even though hash rate is really high, I can still run my miner for the utility it provides, which is heat. I use it to heat the garage that I'm sitting in right now. So in that sense that's how I'm keeping my "business" alive.

Where did this idea come from?

It's a bit of an organic development and a little bit of monkey see monkey do.

After I published my guide and things started heating up in the home mining ecosystem, other people started coming out with their own guides and talking about the ways they did it in their homes. Everybody's got a unique situation, so some people were publishing ways in which they used the heat to heat their home, which for me didn't click at first.

You have to do something with the heat, and I think for most people the heat is a nuisance—at least for me it started out as a nuisance. I didn't need it. Mining profitability was so good when I first started that I didn't have to worry about trying to double-spend energy costs on both Bitcoin and heat. I could just waste the heat. It didn't matter to me because I was accumulating Bitcoin below the going market rate.

Over time, as that changed and it became less profitable to mine Bitcoin, and then it became a total loss to mine Bitcoin at home on my high residential rates, then I started becoming more aware of the importance of regaining any of that ground that I had lost. That's when I started paying more attention to the heat and thinking about ways I could capture it and use it to heat my home.

How do you think about managing your electricity and connectivity?

I think the first thing I'll say is, most homes are wired up to supply 120-volt electricity at the outlets. You may have a couple 240-volt outlets in your home for larger accessories, maybe an electric oven or your electric clothes dryer, but for most people you're going to have to modify your home's electric circuit in some manner in order to get a miner up and running. If you have to do that, consult with a licensed electrician, and if you're not comfortable doing something, or if you don't have the experience to do something that requires a change in your home electric system, don't do it. You'll wind up hurting yourself or hurting others. It's not as expensive as you might think to get the help of a professional where you need it.

Lucky for me, I knew enough to be dangerous, and I had done enough residential electrical work that I was totally confident installing circuit breakers, running electric lines, and installing outlets. To your point about managing electricity with a provider, there are multiple areas of concern that one should pay attention to if privacy is a priority for you. There's your electrical usage footprint, there's your network-level privacy (which is the internet connection), and then there's your on-chain level of privacy from the Bitcoin you're receiving from mining.

When it comes to the electrical company, there's going to be a big spike in constant demand on your home utility bill. That may or may not raise a red flag with your utility company. I'm of the opinion that so long as you're keeping up with your electrical bill, your energy provider is in business to provide energy as a service, and so long as you're paying for that service, they're not going to care what you're doing with it.

Now they may start asking questions when you overload your home's electrical system and wind up melting the overhead lines that run out to their transformer, like I had the unfortunate experience of doing.

You can either make a choice and be upfront with them and tell them that you are mining Bitcoin, or you can try to get clever if you don't want to reveal that detail and say that you're running your own servers or you're running some other high usage electrical equipment. It's for each individual to decide, but for myself I always chose to keep the fact that I was mining Bitcoin private, so when I did set the overhead lines on fire and a technician came out and asked me what happened, I just told him I was running servers, a lot of servers, and I just left it at that.

I tend to keep that information private. Once you put that information out there, you never know what kind of note the electrical company's going to put in your profile, or who's going to look back at that, or how that may come up down the road. I don't think we've really seen the 'then they fight you' stage of Bitcoin, and it could very well be that around the next corner we wake up tomorrow and mining Bitcoin is illegal unless you have a money transmitter license. So the reason I try not to tell any electrical technicians or internet service providers anything about mining Bitcoin is because I'm of the opinion that once you put that information out there, you can't take it back, and you never know how it might get used against you in the future.

That's why I think it's a good idea to keep it to yourself. I don't want this to be construed as everyone should do it the way I did it. I just want to provide insight as to how I did it, and why I did it the way I did, but I want everyone to really think about their own unique circumstances and make the decision that's best for them.

What about privacy in your connectivity?

When it comes to the network-level privacy (i.e., your internet connection), I also wanted that to be as private as possible. Ketan, who operates Ministry of Nodes, put together a good guide that got me started on using a PFSense Router for my home internet. So again, I read what he published, and I took that and did a lot of additional research and documented all my steps, and then I published a guide called "Bitcoin Home Mining Network Privacy." That outlines everything—all the steps I took to secure my network-level privacy.

My concern was that when I connect my miner to the internet, my internet service provider is going to see that. They're going to see the website that I'm connecting to, and they're going to see the traffic because the stratum V1 connection is on unencrypted clearnet, so they're going to know exactly what I'm doing. They're going to know I'm mining Bitcoin if my internet service provider were so inclined to observe what I was doing. That was a concern for me, because in the same way that once you provide information to your utility provider you can't get it back, the same thing is true with your internet service provider.

They log (or have the ability to log) the date, the time, exactly what was in the data packets, what pool you were connecting to, and how long you were connected. They can collect that metadata and put it in your file, and you're never going to know if or when someone with authority asks them to hand over that information or what kind of list you're going to be swept onto for having that information in your file.

It's all about staying off of the lists. I don't want to be on any lists, so in order for me to keep that information private, it became apparent to me that I was going to need a VPN. The VPN was a great solution because it encrypts the data, so it prevents my internet service provider from seeing what data I'm transmitting. Now they can see that it's going to a VPN server, but the internet service provider cannot see where it goes on the other side of that VPN server. They can't definitively conclude what I'm doing because they can't see what's in the traffic, and they can't really see where it's going past the VPN provider.

The other great thing that the VPN does is it solves my second concern with network-level privacy. I didn't want to trust the mining pool in knowing my IP address, because in my opinion, the mining pool could also have the ability to log certain metadata about that connection. They could see the date, the time, the IP address, and the data packets coming in. They know how much hash rate you're providing, and they could make a pretty good guess as to how many miners you're running based on that information.

Depending on the jurisdiction that the mining pool is in, they may or may not be approached by some three-letter agency with the authority at some point to get a sweeping list that contains your IP address and this other metadata about your mining activity. That would give these tyrannical government officials another thread to pull on to then go find which internet service provider was linked to that IP address, and then go dig a little deeper and find personally identifying details about the individual with the account at that ISP linked to that IP address. The VPN prevents the mining pool from seeing what my original IP address is. They can see that my mining connection is coming from a VPN server, but they don't know where it came from prior to that.

What about using the Bitcoin network?

I'm of the opinion that I want to be prepared for the worst and hope for the best. I don't reuse Bitcoin mining reward addresses. A lot of people will set up their Bitcoin mining account and they'll plug in their Bitcoin mining address, and they'll just set it and forget it. They'll receive all of their rewards to the same address. That's bad for privacy, because anyone can look in the public records of the Bitcoin blockchain and see those mining rewards, and if that information ever gets tied to your identity and it ever does become illegal to mine Bitcoin, you're not going to want people you spend your mining rewards with to be able to look back and see that you earned those Bitcoin rewards from a mining pool.

In an uncertain world, I think it's best to adhere to as many privacy best practices as you can, so for Bitcoin network-level privacy, for my own protocol, I started using a different address for every Bitcoin mining payout, which is made really easy in Lincoin, because they've implemented BIP 47, and I can just put my paynym in there, and it automatically generates a fresh Bitcoin address every time I receive a payout. I take it a step further and have all the Bitcoin I get go through Samourai wallet's whirlpool. That is a zero-link coinjoin implementation that will break the deterministic links from where that Bitcoin came from and where it's going. So that way, when I go to spend my Bitcoin in the future, anyone who wants to snoop back through my transaction history will run into this cloud of anonymity that's all like-sized UTXOs. They're not going to be able to determine where exactly my specific UTXO came from prior to that Whirlpool coinjoin.

So what is the future of your business?

We've seen historically how actions and activities that are perfectly legal today could very well be made illegal tomorrow. You may suddenly wake up one day and find yourself on the wrong side of the pendulum and be labeled as a criminal and potentially held accountable for the legal things that you're doing today. I just want to reiterate that I think people should try to preserve as much privacy as they can, whether that be at the physical level, the electrical utility level, the internet connectivity network level, or the Bitcoin network level. Once a person reveals their information, there is no getting it back, so in my opinion private information should be handled with care.

Now I'm also very bullish. I'm very bullish on the innovations that I've seen people producing in the home Bitcoin mining ecosystem. You've got guys who have been producing really clever ways to incorporate Bitcoin mining heat into home heating systems, and different ways to automate that process and control it. For me there's no shortage of innovative ways that the utility of Bitcoin mining will continue to be integrated into the home. I think Bitcoin mining serves a purpose beyond just producing Bitcoin. There's a lot of utility in it.

What do most people misunderstand about Bitcoin mining?

I think most people misunderstand that individuals can do it, and individuals have a lot of different reasons to do it, whether that's accumulating Bitcoin that's not tied to your identity or heating your home. You can mine Bitcoin and it can make a lot of sense for people.

Why does Bitcoin mining matter?

It solves a couple of problems that are very prevalent in the Bitcoin space, like KYC information getting attached to your Bitcoin UTXOs. Mining your own Bitcoin solves that problem, and it solves the problem of permission. You don't have to ask anybody to get involved with it. You can buy a miner, plug it in at home, and start depositing Bitcoin to your own wallet. You don't have to trust any third-party service provider. You don't have to ask for permission from anybody. Those are very important attributes that Bitcoin mining provides.

As we've seen, money has been weaponized to the point that if you don't meet a financial institution's moral standards, you can be shut off from basic financial services with the flip of a switch. It happened to the Canadian trucker convoy, it happens in Communist China with the social credit system. When money gets weaponized, you may be coerced into injecting experimental vaccines into your body against your will, or you may be silenced and hesitant to express your political or religious views. People with contrary opinions are getting punished through the weaponization of money, and when you don't have to ask permission to use money, and when that money is not tied to your identity, then you have the freedom to do what you want to do.

I think securing the individual's freedom is a worthwhile fight.

What final thoughts are important to share, or what have we missed?

I strongly encourage people to do their own research and use critical thinking skills to the best of their ability to figure out if mining is right for them or not. I encourage them to try, because I think most people are going to find it's not as difficult as they might think. They're going to find that there's a lot of upside to having unidentified permissionless money, and they're going to learn some additional skills along the way.

You're going to learn something about electrical, HVAC, carpentry, and networking. I think the more people we have learning how to use their hands and their critical thinking skills, and the more those people have censorship-resistant permissionless money, is how we start building a better world that we can leave to our children.

I'll leave you with one hot take prediction to ruffle some feathers: The days are numbered for companies that have built a business on mining Bitcoin alone. In order for Bitcoin mining businesses to survive, they will certainly have to vertically integrate other services that support mining (or the mining will have to support the additional services they provide). In either case, I predict that the days of vanilla Bitcoin mining companies are gone for good.

Rick Vanderhulst: Open Sourcing Home Mining for Heat with 3D Printing

It is said that necessity is the mother of invention. In this case, necessity also has 3D design skills and their own manufacturing business. What started as a personal project to replace a space heater with an S9 to keep his wife warm on chilly winter nights evolved into a home heater that has put mining setups into hundreds of homes.

As the founder and CEO of CryptoCloaks, Rick Vanderhulst may be most readily known for his iconic Bitcoin grenades and custom 3D printed node cases, but rising in popularity are his designs within the home mining ecosystem. He has designed, printed, and optimized various intakes, exhaust shrouds, and customizable cases that allow miners to retrofit their machines for use in the home. This rapid prototyping, combined with an open-source ethos, has turbocharged innovation in home mining while embracing the "Freedom Money" culture of Bitcoin.

Who are you and how did you find yourself in Bitcoin mining?

My name is Rick Vanderhulst. I run a 3D printing business in the Bitcoin space that over the past few years has grown a side division for Bitcoin mining. Everybody knows the usual story. You start by going down these sh*tcoin rabbit holes gambling to make money, then you realize how unique Bitcoin is. You just want to learn more and more about it. To me, the basics start with running your own node, then everybody wants to start tinkering with Bitcoin mining. At least that was my path.

So my first machine was really how I got started in this whole thing, and why I started building products for home mining. I started running an S9 in my house, just to understand the basics of Bitcoin mining, learning all about pools, hash rate, stuff like that. I started tinkering, and then as time went on, I figured, "Well, there's got to be more ways we can run these machines," and that's where it all began.

What is your business?

My business is CryptoCloaks. We're a 3D printing and design company. We started from one tiny 3D-printed mount that held a hardware wallet underneath your desk to keep it out of sight. From there we branched out into different products throughout the Bitcoin space, from node cases and mounts for other hardware wallets to fun items like our Bitcoin grenades. What really started up two years ago was our interest in the Bitcoin mining space and how to design and build efficiencies in mining.

There were a lot of questions on how Bitcoin miners could run machines in their homes. That really hit home with me because that was one of my latest passions. There's about a billion things that you can do just with the heat itself, and everything branched off from that. I had an S9—that was my first machine—so I wanted to start using that in the wintertime to heat my garage to keep our cars warm. My second miner was an S19. With that, I wanted to take the S19 and heat my entire house. That was a matter of "How can I take the heat from the S19 and actually pump it in my ductwork?"

There are awesome Telegram groups that brought these ideas to the forefront, and since my company is 3D printing and design, I was able to take the ideas and bring them to life. That's where our home mining division really got started for the business. We created fan shrouds to clip or screw on to the back of the miners. From there, we could take the heat from the exhaust side and bring it into an 8-inch or 6-inch duct and connect it to your home heating system.

Where did this idea come from?

When you have a miner running, you have to do something with the heat. And if you run it in your house, you're obviously going to heat up your house. In the wintertime, it's great. It's free heat, and you're getting paid back in Bitcoin. For me, I liked the no KYC aspect as well. I don't have to buy Bitcoin from an exchange. I mine it and put it into cold storage. Nobody ever has to see what happens to it. But there is always a problem in the summertime. What do you do with the heat?

In my system, I have it hooked up to where the miner heats the house to a certain temperature. I have a probe that goes through my floor from the basement into the living room. That connects to a temperature box that has two outlets on it and switches based on the temperature. Once the temperature hits 73 degrees, one intake fan stops pulling air into the house and the cold side would start to exhaust excess heat outside of the house. That way you never overheat your house. I designed a shroud that allowed me to exhaust efficiently with ducting, so I can actually connect everything together instead of having two big fans blow into or out of the basement.

How do you manage your connectivity and electricity?

For connectivity there's two different ways for our S9 space heater cases. We have an option where you can use your regular ethernet cord and an option to use plug-in Wi-Fi adapters so you don't have to worry about extra cables going into your wall sockets. For the electricity aspect, there's a ton of different ways you can manage that. On our space heater designs, we like to do 650 watts on our miners, where we don't burn a lot of electricity and can use a normal 110v outlet. It uses less power than an actual space heater—probably by half. You still heat your home, and you get paid back in Bitcoin, KYC-free, so you don't have to worry about privacy.

What is this space heater you're referring to?

The S9 space heater. It's a fully open-source project we did about a year and a half ago. In my bedroom we had a 1500-watt electric space heater. My wife was always getting cold at night, and she wanted it on and running for 8 to 10 hours. I looked at that and thought, "Why the hell do we have this when we could easily use an S9 to heat the same room?" The biggest factor was noise. Miners are loud as hell, so we had to take into account the noise of the fans. How could we mitigate that and make them quieter and what I call "wife proof."

We started looking at different fan options, because you can swap out the original fans from the S9. We did a large-scale test of various model fans with data plots on the decibel readings at different wattages. We tested up to the point where the miner overheated. We found settings that we liked most in the bedroom, and the wife was happy. That was 650 watts, and the decibel readings were only 42 DB, which was actually less than the regular space heater, which was around 48 to 50 DB. The best part is now you get to mine Bitcoin in your house. You heat your room, just like you normally would, and you're actually running half the wattage of a regular space heater.

That's our most exciting project in the Bitcoin mining space over the last two years, and it has really taken off. It's open-sourced. Anybody can print the cases. Anybody can print the adapters to attach the fans. There's a full 30-page guide where the build process is broken down into steps so anyone can easily build it themselves. It's amazing to see the uses the community has already discovered with the space heaters. That's what we're most excited about—a space heater miner in every household.

What is the future of your business?

Hopefully we can have heaters in more and more houses. With next-generation miners, there's a lot of action going on, like where you take one single hashboard and you run it off of 110 volts. This is done with a Loki board from Zach Bomsta. The creators and the tinkerers are really taking it to the next level and make it more efficient to have space heaters. We're also going to keep designing shrouds for the next-generation miners that come out. We still produce shrouds for S9s, and we open-sourced a lot of those designs so people can print themselves.

Bitcoin mining is supposed to be decentralized and we want to give all the plebs at home the chance to print their own so they don't always have to buy them. It goes with the mantra of Bitcoin as freedom money. We want to keep giving products out that people can print themselves. They can design and do whatever they want.

What do most people misunderstand about Bitcoin mining?

That it's easy. A lot of people think that Bitcoin mining is an easy thing to do, or they're always going to make out like a bandit. I think people get greedy and see other facilities and how they make money. I remember buying two S19s for $12,000 each, and a year later they were going for $1,200. When people first buy their miner, they expect that they're going to pay it off. That's probably not going to happen. It takes a lot of different factors and cheap electricity to really break even, when in hindsight you could just stack sats.

We bought miners because we wanted to prototype, so we needed the units themselves, and also to heat the house while doing it. One big factor people need to remember is that it's not easy money. You're probably better off stacking sats if you can't pay off the price of buying the miner and doing something with the heat.

Why does Bitcoin mining matter?

Bitcoin mining is one of *the* most important things. It decentralizes the network, and it keeps attack vectors at bay by costing too much money. For me, Bitcoin mining is my niche. Since two years ago, when we created the home mining division of CryptoCloaks, it really has become one of my bigger passions. I always want to create new ideas, new products, and try to bring them to more and more people. In general that's why I did the original space heater design, and people are loving it. I want as many people as possible to run miners in their homes. It helps decentralize the network and helps people get non-KYC Bitcoin. I think that's truly important. Everybody should have at least an S9 or some kind of miner running in their home so you can have true freedom money. Trading electricity no matter the cost for Bitcoin is a good enough reason for me.

What final thoughts are important to share, or what have we missed?

Everyone should at least run an S9 in their house. I think it's super important. You will help decentralize the entire network to fight off these giant farms and corporations that are running hundreds of thousands of miners. It's the plebs chance to step up and help decentralize the network. It's really not that expensive. For less than $2 to $3 a day you can run an S9, under clocked at 400 to 650 watts, and fight the system. That way we don't ever have to worry about one major corporation running all of the miners and having a shot at a 51% attack. It probably will never happen, but you never know.

That's why we're here, right? We don't want corporations to run everything; we don't want the government to run everything. It's the people's money, so step your game up. Get a miner and help decentralize the network.

Jason Les: Mega-mining, Grid Stabilization, and a Future of Energy Abundance

It would be easy to assume that size is all that matters in Bitcoin mining. That the biggest operators with the most expansive farms and the largest electrical capacities obsolete mining at all other scales. Jason Les, CEO of Riot Platforms, paints a different picture.

What began as his fascination with Bitcoin code and the hardware that makes it possible evolved into his ascension to the head of a publicly traded company with the largest known single-site Bitcoin mine in the world.

Jason paints for us his vision of mega mining as a tool to reduce energy waste and stabilize grid-level operations for electrical providers. He sees a future of energy abundance, where the oft-attacked mechanism of proof-of-work is embraced as a feature and not a bug. By integrating with energy systems from production to generation and deep downstream to consumption, Bitcoin mining has the opportunity to serve both the incredibly large and the incredibly small miner. This empowers both the Bitcoin network and a monetary future of freedom and human flourishing.

Who are you and how did you find yourself in Bitcoin mining?

My name is Jason Les. I'm the CEO of Riot Platforms. I first found my way into Bitcoin in 2013 and then Bitcoin mining in 2016. As I started to learn more and more about how Bitcoin works, I became very interested in getting involved in it hands-on. I was interested from both a software and hardware perspective. From a software perspective, I was doing a number of programming projects around Bitcoin, trying to understand how Bitcoin worked at the lowest possible level I could understand. I've been around computers my whole life, and I think anyone involved in computers loves getting new things, building computers, and building different kinds of systems.

The idea that I could take this software and get involved in a hands-on way with hardware was super interesting to me. Naturally, the easiest way to do that was GPU mining. I figured, I have a pretty good computer, I can just start mining. I started scaling up operations, always small, just in the space that I had available. I was building GPU rigs, then eventually building with S9s.

Being able to get involved in the space with hardware by building things was rewarding for me. I really wasn't trying to make a lot of money doing it. I built my models and thought, "Okay, if this all works out, I can make some money," but I just spent countless hours building, finding out problems, figuring out how to make things better. That was fun, and that led me to develop more and more expertise around mining. When Riot became a Bitcoin company in 2017, I was asked to join the advisory board because of my technical background and my experience in the mining space.

Take us back to that first machine you ran. Tell us about it.

I think it was five GeForce GPUs in an open-air rig. The Bitcoin talk forums have so much information to help you. That's what is so cool about the space—people are sharing what they're doing. I could read through the forums, watch videos, and see how people were doing things, then find different components that made things easier. I was throwing it together like that.

What is your business?

Riot Platforms is a vertically integrated Bitcoin mining company, which means we not only buy and operate Bitcoin miners, but we build and operate our own infrastructure. We own our own electrical engineering and manufacturing divisions. In our experience, we found it very important to own and control as many of the inputs to our business as possible. Of course, that only goes so far, but the more we're able to control, the more risk we're able to reduce, and the more competitive we are. Our objective is to mine Bitcoin for the lowest price possible, which gives us the most leverage on the upside of Bitcoin.

We want to multiply efficiency to the greatest scale. If we're effectively buying Bitcoin at $5,500 a coin, we want to scale up as much as possible to be able to maximize our financial upside. Also, from a capital perspective, we have found that being a large miner, and being a publicly traded miner, gives us valuable access to capital. That lets us build a lot bigger than others. Having access to public capital markets has been a huge advantage. Because we've been in this industry for so long, we're one of the first public miners, and because of the scale we operate at, we're an exciting story—a story that people are interested in investing in.

To be publicly traded requires a good amount of corporate overhead that private miners won't require. Overhead in terms of cost, in terms of people, in terms of systems and processes, things we have to think about that private miners don't have to worry about. Now that we have performance results, we can raise capital easily, but we have all of this extra work that we have to do. That's another reason why we need sufficient scale—to cover all of that additional overhead and complexity that we have. From our corporate perspective, access to capital by being a large publicly traded miner is critically important.

Where did this idea and strategy of scale come from?

I'll talk about the evolution of the company. When Riot started out, it was doing a number of things. The core business was Bitcoin mining, but it was also making investments in the space. It was looking at launching an exchange in the US; it was looking at building a mining pool. Over time, we narrowed our focus to specifically Bitcoin, and specifically Bitcoin mining. We had the experience of Bitcoin mining. That was the best way that we saw to get exposure to Bitcoin, and that was our core belief—that Bitcoin was the future.

At that time we had a 12-megawatt facility in Oklahoma. It's crazy how the industry grows. When we first acquired that facility in early 2018, that was big; 12 megawatts was big back then. We were operating, I think it was 250 petahash of S9s. In my mind, we were a real player, but Bitcoin mining is always a game of scale, so we needed a way to continue to grow. But we couldn't grow any further at that site. It was using old industrial space for Bitcoin mining, so it wasn't built exactly the way we wanted to build it. Cooling was very difficult, electricity pricing wasn't amazing (especially during the summer), so we decided we needed to move to continue to grow.

We then moved to a third-party hosting facility called Coinmint. We moved all our miners there and bought new miners and sent them there. That was a way for us to continue to grow, but we still hadn't achieved what we desired. We wanted to be vertically integrated. We wanted more control. We saw what was happening in Texas, and we wanted to be a part of demonstrating the value of Bitcoin mining on the grid, so we needed extensive access to power. We needed a large facility to expand from, and we needed a team to do it. At that time, the company was only five people, relying on Coinmint (our third-party host) for operations.

So we started searching. We looked at building everything from scratch, and we looked at buying existing facilities. That led us to acquiring Whinstone US in May of 2021. Now we have one of the lowest-cost PPAs, a team, and site capacity. The story here is that we started off focused on being a part of building a Bitcoin future in that small facility in Oklahoma, then to a third-party host, and now to owning our own facilities. We no longer have to pay that extra hosting fee, which can be a lot, especially when you're paying a profit share during a bull market. Today we want to control our inputs and be a part of the power opportunity here in Texas.

How do you think about managing your inputs?

Power is the number one input to focus on. That's where we spend a lot of our focus, thinking about the ideal locations to get power and at a competitive price. Other things can ultimately be solved for anywhere we're looking. Heat is certainly a challenge. We have had our own challenges, and we're learning from them. But it's ultimately power that's going to be the input that's going to be the most critical for us. That is the number one priority, and that's what we're always focused on.

What is the future of your business?

Our vision for the future is that Bitcoin mining will be integrated with electrical infrastructure. The advantage that it adds to stabilizing energy grids, monetizing stranded and surplus energy, and different types of generators really solves a major inefficiency for mankind. We waste one-third of the energy that's generated globally. It's lost in transmission and curtailed. That is a major inefficiency that we have as a society, and Bitcoin mining is the first large-scale tool that fits all of the criteria required to solve that problem in an efficient way.

In the future, I think you're going to see Bitcoin mining as a load on the grid that's helping stabilize supply and demand as a tool for grid operators. I think you're going to see it paired with generation all over the place, so generators are maximizing their financial potential as well. That is the future that we're trying to build here, and at our stage now, we are demonstrating that on the grid level. We operate the largest controllable load resource in the world and participate in demand response at a scale, I believe, beyond anyone else in the industry.

That is a gradually then suddenly story, just like Bitcoin itself. Bitcoin gradually and then suddenly consumes both individual interest and then popular interest. The first part is what we're still going through right now. We are in the gradual phase of understanding and appreciating Bitcoin mining as an energy tool. Once you cross over the 'suddenly' chasm, it will be impossible to compete in energy without being involved in Bitcoin mining.

What do most people misunderstand about Bitcoin mining?

The biggest misunderstanding is a broad societal belief that using energy is bad. Using energy is linked to the flourishing of humanity. Human lifespan, comfort in living, the technology we use to maximize our productivity, all of this comes as a result of using energy. The internet uses a lot of energy, but connects everyone to share data. That's simple, yet you share data all over the world in a way that you couldn't even conceive of 100 years ago. Bitcoin mining is the next evolution of using energy to improve humanity.

We're using energy to distribute and secure a new form of money globally, so just as the internet uses energy to transform how people share information, Bitcoin is using energy to transform how people use and exchange money, which is a very important mechanism. Money is the purest form of communication, because people's spending generally reflects their honest intentions and beliefs. They buy the things they want, they sell the things they don't want anymore. It's one of the more honest forms of communication.

I think the idea that Bitcoin mining uses energy and that energy use is for nothing is a major misconception. People are like, "Oh, it's just running formulas, it doesn't do anything." It is running a hash function, but doing that is what makes Bitcoin work. This is what has solved the problem that makes Bitcoin possible. I think one of the challenges is people hear about proof of stake, and they're like, "Why can't we just do that? You're not using energy."

Debating how Bitcoin works requires a lot more knowledge about this space, which is challenging. I've sat with members of Congress who bring up proof of stake, and then suddenly I'm having to try to talk with this person about consensus mechanisms, and how consensus is achieved in Bitcoin, and now we're in so much detail. What's a node? Okay, how does a node impact consensus versus miners? That's way too much nuance and it becomes difficult to make the point. So that's a challenge.

Getting back to your question on the misconceptions. The misconception is that using energy is bad, and Bitcoin uses energy for no reason, and it's an inefficient use of energy, like it's a design flaw or something. That's what we have to educate people about. Bitcoin is a technical thing, and its valuable properties come from a technical explanation. If someone gives very novice critiques, like asking, "How do you know there's only 21 million?" Well, because it's in the code. "How do you know who controls it?" Now you're down the rabbit hole. People want to understand how consensus works, how private-public cryptography works, all of it.

It's a challenge because it's money. With the internet, it's not that you have to understand how the internet works to send an email or look at a website. With money the stakes are much higher and people have a more natural skepticism.

What I often say to people is that Bitcoin has this interesting way of making people understand the world around them more. First, let's just start at the money level. When you start learning about Bitcoin, you start thinking about fiat money in a way you never thought about before. Most people in the Bitcoin community are talking about inflation and access to money, and it's a very top-of-mind thing. The fact is, most people are going through the day and they're not thinking about inflation. They don't think about how their money is stored, and their true ownership over transmitting that money. They're just going through the day, going through the motions, and don't have to think about it.

Then you discover Bitcoin and you start questioning, and you're learning more about the world—a major part of it you didn't think about before. Then you get down to Bitcoin mining, and now you're thinking about energy grids and how power works in a way that you never thought about before. Bitcoin has this transformative effect with the system itself. It forces people to learn more about these critical parts of the world around them that they did not give any bandwidth to before.

What final thoughts are important to share, or what have we missed?

There are people who are concerned that the big miners are going to be the dominant player and complete consolidated the mining space. Tying it back to the vision that we talked about—of Bitcoin mining being integrated with energy infrastructure—there are going to be all sizes of capacity available all over the place. People can monetize excess capacity at their home, bigger capacity in some industrial spaces, small generation or very large scale like Riot does. We're all filling a different need, and what we are all doing is converting energy into Bitcoin. I've heard people talk about Bitcoin as energy money. It's the ability to take energy and convert it to Bitcoin, and the cheaper price you're getting energy for, the cheaper your Bitcoin is.

At Riot, we're doing this on a large scale, and we're trying to work with counterparties on a large scale to demonstrate the value of Bitcoin and act upon the different opportunities that Bitcoin is bringing to us. We are one piece of the mining land-scape for Bitcoin. We're not mutually exclusive to others. What makes Bitcoin more robust, secure, and distributed is not just that we have large-scale miners putting so much power into Bitcoin, but the fact there are so many miners of different scales as a part of this equation. I personally think that will always be the case. There's always going to be different sizes, different levels of capacity, and power available. Different profiles of miners will come to reach them. The fact there is this low barrier to entry for mining, and that these different types of capacities exist, is what drives the decentralization and security of Bitcoin.

Erik Hersman: Electro-Optimism and a Mission to Empower 1.1 Billion People

Electricity is directly correlated to human flourishing, but in the developed world, we take that for granted. The alarm goes off in the morning, you scroll social media while making your coffee, and grab the bread and butter from the refrigerator for a quick snack before work. What would have taken you tens of minutes or an hour one hundred and fifty years ago and involved stoking a fire or collecting water now happens immediately and almost invisibly.

The modern world is here and we don't even think about it.

Much of the world does not have this luxury, and Erik Hersman, serial African entrepreneur, is working to change that. What began as technological curiosity and a desire to generate Bitcoin himself developed into Gridless, a company with the goal of electrifying hundreds of millions of individuals on the African continent. By using Bitcoin mining as a buyer of both first and last resort on remote electrical infrastructure, Erik and his team help make energy projects both viable to build and sustainable to operate. His model maintains sovereignty for African businesses and communities and plants the seeds of human flourishing and abundance across the developing world.

Who are you and how did you find yourself in Bitcoin mining?

My name is Erik Hersman. I, alongside my partners Phillip Walton and Janet Maingi, have been building a company called Gridless. I grew up in Kenya and Sudan and have been in the software and hardware space in Africa for many years now. I actually looked at Bitcoin mining back in 2011. I was running a place called the iHub in Nairobi, and we had a supercomputer cluster that we built. I'd been thinking it would be interesting if we used some of the spare cycles at night and on weekends to mine Bitcoin—times where it wasn't being used by people in the community. We never did it. We looked again at mining in 2013 or 2014, since there was a massive 400-megawatt wind farm put up in Northern Kenya, where they were dumping power directly into the ground because they had not designed it with transmission. They wouldn't have transmission for the next five to six years.

We thought about it, but we had just founded a new company. We said, "No, we've got to focus on what we are supposed to be building right now." In 2016 I started looking at Bitcoin again. I was going to buy myself ten S9s and plug them in at the office, because energy was included in our bill. We ended up getting a deal on a really nice piece of property in Kenya, so I ended up buying some property instead. Then finally, this last time, we were selling our last company, I was like, "You know what—I'm going to do something in Bitcoin."

The last company was about building hardware and then deploying it as the connectivity infrastructure for rural and urban internet in Africa. Philip and I were looking at that and talking to Janet, and we said, "Listen, instead of building another software company, why don't we build this hardware company? We're maybe some of the best-placed people in Africa, with the best resumes for this kind of thing." Bitcoin mining is actually simpler than what we used to do. The mining machines are not that intelligent. That's what finally got us into mining after well over a decade of not doing mining—digging down into it and really understanding it.

I should add that in 2020 I spent a good deal of time reading. I never had a conviction on Bitcoin because I hadn't done the reading and learning. When I finally dug down into it and I understood how it was different from other cryptocurrencies, as well as why proof-of-work was so important, that's when we decided to go into Bitcoin and specifically Bitcoin mining.

Do you remember the first machines you ran? Tell us about them.

The first machines we picked up were S17s, but they were just complete crap. They were used S17s, which are maybe the worst of the worst, because S17s were not reliable anyway. It was just three of us, and we're sitting there trying to get hash boards working again and breaking these things down for repairs. Luckily, we had a background in hardware, so we were able to take them apart, jump into both the power supply side as well as the hash boards, and fix things. But they still didn't last very long.

Then we said, "Let's go ahead and get some financing behind this company and do it." There's something special here, and I think the reason why there's something special here plays out in two ways. It is a really interesting way to be involved in Bitcoin at a very low level, and potentially have access to Bitcoin at a cheaper rate than it would be in the future, and it's also interesting because in Africa there are different dynamics we have around energy, and Bitcoin mining can play a special role. The more we talked to the people who were building the energy, the more we realized we should do this.

You're alluding to your business. What is it?

At first we thought Gridless was going to be a Bitcoin mining company, and it is. That's what we do—our goal is to make money by mining Bitcoin. But what we found out over the intervening year and a half since we started the company is that it's actually an energy company too. It's much more about energy than it is about running a data center. The data center is simple in a way. It's a bunch of dumb computers, lined up on a rack, connected to the internet. You then connect a big fat power plug in from the power partner and away you go. We put this in a 20-foot container that we build right here in Nairobi.

We deploy that container to the site where the power is. Right next to a powerhouse, generally speaking, and we put that big cable into the side of it, and that's all the work that our power partner has to do. We do everything from there. We set up the mining container. We set up all of the miners. We do all the network connectivity. We put in a special ruggedized micro-server, which is what we built in our last company, so we know it really well. That device is the brains of the whole outfit.

We flip the switch, and we turn them all on, and then depending on how much power is being used by the community of people who are getting power from that same power company, or businesses getting power from that power company, we turn on or off machines remotely and automatically. We call that demand leveling. We are the real-time demand leveler for that power grid in that rural African community. We've done this in three countries—we're in Kenya, Malawi, and Zambia—and we have six sites. We have primarily hydropower, but we've also branched into geothermal, which has a solar component to it, and then biomass as well, which is vegetable matter or biomatter that is burned.

Where did this idea come from?

When we started Gridless, we were coming in as buyers of last resort to the power partner. We were walking in saying, "Okay, what's your leftover wasted energy that's not going anywhere and you can't make any money off of?" Most of these power partners are sitting at anywhere between 20% to 40% of their power used and 60 to 80% wasted or stranded power. We come in and say, "Do you want to use the full capacity that you have?" If you do, and you want to make some money off of that, then you can get a revenue share with us from the Bitcoin that we generate. What became interesting was when we started talking to some of our partners who wanted to build new sites. They needed a buyer of first resort, somebody who would walk in with them at the very beginning and be the anchor tenant until they started to get a local community and businesses onto that power.

Bitcoin mining is interesting because it comes in these little shoe boxes that are each three kilowatts a piece in approximate power usage. That means that you can turn on or off three kilowatts at a time. You don't make money if you've turned them off, but you don't lose money when you turn them off either. So unlike other industrial off-takers of energy, we can turn things off very granularly in a way that most others can't, and we can ramp them up very quickly too. There's no other industry that can do that, and that makes us a really good partner for somebody who's building out energy. They all of a sudden have 100% capacity usage from day one, which completely changes their financials.

We hadn't understood how energy guys raised money before. It's this willing fiction between the energy developer and the energy investor in mini grids in Africa. They think they're going to go from 20% usage in the first year, to 40% in the next couple years, to 80% by year eight, and then 100% from year ten onwards, and they're going to get their return on investment in 30 years' time. None of them do. They get to maybe 20% or 40% usage and that's it.

The reason is simple. People don't use energy at night. They're asleep, and they turn the power off. It also takes a while for people to go from buying their first LED light bulb and charging their phone to buying a refrigerator and a TV. So there's this fiction that everybody plans around in the energy space about energy usage. They run off with their numbers like it's real when it doesn't actually happen that way. Where Bitcoin mining becomes interesting for everybody doing energy across the continent is that from day one, whether you're putting in 20 Bitcoin miners in a small box or cabinet or you're putting in 144 machines with a 500 kilowatt 20-foot mining container, you can immediately take up the full excess amount and monetize it—even while you're trying to fulfill the mission of electrifying Africa.

Why is that important?

It's important because by electrifying Africa, you're electrifying a little bit over half of the 1.1 billion people who don't have power in the world. If you want to see Africa take part in the 21st century global economy, then we need to have power and we need to have connectivity. There's a good mission behind what people are trying to do with energy developments, but most of the time it doesn't have the financial numbers that back it up. Bitcoin mining comes to fill that gap. Very few people wanted to believe that Bitcoin mining could be helpful, but it has been. You can see the differences on both the balance sheets and on the faces of our power partners around Africa. We realized that while we do this to make Bitcoin, the way we do it is by providing an offtaker for energy to be built and be financially viable across the continent.

What is the future of your business?

Africa today is not the Africa of the 80s and 90s that everybody remembers or sees on TV. I think that sometimes it's hard for people, because what you see on TV is either people running races or safaris, or it's a slum or a story about a civil war in a country. You get these big-picture stories, but it doesn't really break down into the reality of what it's like to actually live and work and build in Africa. Africa is much more nuanced than that. It's 54 countries, it's multiple languages. You have advanced cultures and societies, and you have ones that are more rural and still catching up. You have this wide swath of experiences.

The goal of Gridless is to mine Bitcoin. That's simply what we do. The *mission* that we're on is about helping to decentralize the Bitcoin network by making sure that Bitcoin mining happens in other parts of the world and to help electrify Africa.

On the first point, we help decentralize the Bitcoin network, but we have to be careful that we don't become just another big miner owning the hash in Africa. There should be more people and companies across Africa doing the same thing. With that in mind, about a year ago, we helped start GAMA, which is the Green Africa Mining Alliance. That's an organization that has six different companies in it, from Ethiopia and Nigeria to Kenya, Congo, and Zambia. Countries where there's Bitcoin mining happening, and people who are now networked with each other, trying to use each other as a community to help further the ideas by training new people into Bitcoin mining. All of us are small businesses.

Second, we've started what we call The Seed Program, where we provide refurbished and low-priced miners to new miners who want to get going in Africa. That way they can be seeded and start to mine and have a community of people who will help them get started without making all the same mistakes that we did initially. We already have one of our GAMA Partners, who started off with just a couple Bitcoin miners in rural Nigeria, now running a couple hundred kilowatts of Bitcoin miners. You can start from nothing and grow. Not everybody has the right connections to know where to buy miners from, know which ones to buy, know who to buy them from, know how to set them up, etc.

For example, in Africa, Bitmain miners like S19s can't handle the environmental issues that we have here—the heat, the dust, the bugs, those kinds of things. Whatsminers from MicroBT do a much better job. Not making the mistake of buying Bitmain, but buying MicroBT instead is a really important starting point so you don't trip and fall on your face too quickly. Bitcoin mining can be hard, and it can be a brutal space to be in. You don't need extra roadblocks. GAMA is about that, but why bring that up as the strategy of Gridless?

We don't want to be the behemoth of Africa. We want to be a good-sized Bitcoin mining company in Africa, but we want to be one of many. Number one, we make sure that we're not the only target for legislative bodies in different jurisdictions, but also it doesn't help the Bitcoin mining network if we're just another big mining company sitting here in Africa.

Having said that, our strategy is to continue doing this community and smaller-scale Bitcoin mining across multiple geographies. That helps derisk us and ensure that there's groups of others that are also willing to do the same type of thing. We would rather have 20 sites across Africa that are 500 kilowatts to three megawatts each than to have a single 100-megawatt site in one country. We think that the geographic spread is useful for Bitcoin as well as de-risking the company.

What do most people misunderstand about Bitcoin mining?

They think it's hard. Mining is actually simple. There's some complexity in it, and the complexities don't scale linearly as you grow. Bitcoin mining gets logarithmically more difficult with more nuance the larger you grow. Running three miners in your basement is super easy. Just get a miner and go do it. The 'Mining for the Streets' mentality behind it is perfect. Use your power company as a proxy for getting KYC-free Bitcoin. Nobody should stop or blink too much about that. It's just not complex. Going from that to 100 miners sitting in a container has added complexity. You've got network complexity and you're using larger amounts of power. That's not just complex but more dangerous. It's the same thing when you go from 100 Bitcoin miners in a 20ft container to 1,000 or 20,000 miners sitting in a warehouse. Now the scale of difficulty and nuance increases. Just the networking side alone takes a specialist.

I don't think the simplicity of Bitcoin mining is fully appreciated. Anytime we look at a mechanical object, we at first go, "What's inside that box?" Our imagination runs a little bit wild, but if you can just get to a place that has a miner, you can look at it, see it, and demystify it to yourself, and you quickly realize how easy it is to get going.

What else is important to share, or what have we missed?

We came into mining in the bear market of 2022, and what was interesting about that is we started to look at the historical data on Bitcoin mining and energy price. We realized there's a really interesting thing about that historical data. We looked at five years of Bitcoin mining at a dollar per kilowatt basis, and Bitcoin mining pays out around 8 to 9 cents per kilowatt. It fluctuates. It'll spike up, and it doesn't ever go down below 6 cents.

Really what we should do is abstract ourselves a level away from the Bitcoin price. What we should be thinking is that there are certain times and certain places where we actually need to be running low-efficiency and not high-efficiency settings on these miners. We're not making as much Bitcoin, but it does make us a financially viable company. That viability is important to us, because it means that we cover ourselves for the downsides of the market, even though we might reduce some of our upside on Bitcoin earned.

There's a habit people have of buying machines that are the most terahash they can possibly buy and not thinking about how much energy is being spent to run that machine. In the future, joules per terahash are going to be much more important. Our abstraction allows us to look at joules per terahash very seriously. We've been doing that for a year now, and that way of modeling and understanding what Bitcoin mining as a small business can do allowed us to think through our algorithms for which miners go on or off, which ones are at high efficiency, and which ones are at low efficiency. I think it's important that people understand when you buy machines, you might need to be running these things in a low-efficiency setting, or you might need to be running in a high-efficiency setting, and depending on what you're going to be doing, you'll choose a certain type of machine. I think we might be past the phase of everybody just looking at the most terahash per Bitcoin miner. Instead, I think we're going to be looking at efficiency.

What else might the future bring?

This is more important for emerging markets than it is for emerged markets. I think that the future of energy generation will be tied to Bitcoin mining, and that Bitcoin mining can actually be *the* financing tool to build new energy. In our part of the world, the finances just don't work for a smaller-sized power site to be built. They're 100% unviable unless you're trying to sell to the grid at some high price. If you're trying to electrify new places, it just doesn't work. However, with Bitcoin mining leading the charge, you can actually make the numbers work really well.

Where it used to take say 30 years to get a return on investment, now you can have that ROI in five to seven years with Bitcoin mining bolted on as the primary user of that energy while the community ramps up over the intervening years.

We have this fear, uncertainty, and doubt around Bitcoin, which ends up muddying the perception of it. They're saying, "Oh, Bitcoin is bad for x or y," but the truth is that Bitcoin mining is both a net positive for energy and something that can further humanity's progress. This sounds very hyperbolic, but it's not—it's actually true. If you want to see people move forward, go turn on electricity in a village that doesn't have it.

When the sun goes down in these communities, it gets very dark very quickly. If you can turn on a light, you can add security. You can add the ability to irrigate fields. You can add the ability for hospitals to stay on and open. You can add the ability for the hospital to have cold storage. You can add the ability for young kids to be able to study at night and not have to be around a kerosene lantern or a wood-burning stove messing up their lungs. It has a massive effect on human progress. Energy is that base layer that everybody needs to move forward. If we take away the anti-Bitcoin marketing hype that's out there, what we see is a tool that can change the future for huge swaths of the global population.

The difference between those who have energy and those who don't is a massive divide that nobody benefits from. The rest of the people on the globe don't benefit from people not having energy in rural Malawi. The people in rural Malawi, when they can get electricity for the first time, can increase their GDP, which is not a zero-sum game to everybody else in the world. When those young kids grow up, and they're on the internet, or people start making goods, services, and products that are exported around the world, those things are all net benefits for the globe. It means progress. There's nobody who doesn't benefit from this.

CONCLUSION

In **nine short** pages (including citations), the Bitcoin whitepaper details the structures and mechanisms of the peer-to-peer electronic cash system we know today. Yet nowhere in this seminal document will you find the modern Bitcoin mining machine, the mining pool, joules per terahash, containerized mining, or a slew of other industry-standard inventions. You won't find a discussion on mega-mining, a how-to guide for machine operation, or a set of models to detail profit maximization as a Bitcoin miner.

When you read old BitcoinTalk forum discussions, Satoshi has little to say about the hardware side of mining, the potential to incentivize energy generation, or the opportunities to consume and monetize waste products. Never did Satoshi detail a thesis around the business of Bitcoin mining. They seem to have given us the core incentives of our industry and allowed us to figure out the rest.

This puts the Bitcoin mining industry in a distinctly different position than the Bitcoin software industry. While development arguments rage around which OP code should be activated or which use of scripting is a spam attack on the network, you are unlikely to find miners infighting about the best methods of machine cooling or how to establish profitable business models.

This divide reduces to a key difference between the worlds of software and hardware. Software exists "in-here" and lives on the node of every self-sovereign Bitcoiner, while hardware lives "out-there" and lives or dies on its own merits in the field.

To be a Bitcoin miner requires no review process, no BIP submissions or approvals. But to be a successful software developer requires contributing code that achieves a degree of proficiency few can master. Software conversations are intricate and deeply nuanced, often hearkening to seminal documents (like the Bitcoin whitepaper) and historical precedent recorded in earlier technical submissions.

In this sense Bitcoin mining is for the many, and for that reason is experiencing a Cambrian explosion of innovation in both technology and business type. While the world of Bitcoin "in-here" must be clean, error-free, and always compile, the world of Bitcoin "out-there" is a necessary grudge match, a true Wild West where innovators stake claims and move mountains, with some surviving on their wits alone and others dying due only to bad luck or timing. Bitcoin miners are more like Darwin's finches or ancient megafauna than we may think, often living and dying at the mercy of nothing more than the vicissitudes of the world around us.

In the world of systems thinking, there is a heuristic coined by Stafford Beer called POSIWID: The Purpose of a System is What it Does.[71] Maybe this best explains the position we occupy within the mining industry. Bitcoiners that work "in-here" on development, self-custody, exchanges, or other tech advances often ask themselves if their work aligns with the vision of Bitcoin as a system. Do their design choices maximize decentralization, permissionlessness, and privacy? They participate not only in the technological aspect of Bitcoin but also the political. Their choices may align them with—or distract them from—the developing ethos of Bitcoin.

But a Bitcoin miner operates under a slightly different ethos, and has a more primary question to ask themselves. *Is my operation profitable?* This forces the miner to live practically, and to always match their head in the clouds dreaming with boots on the ground execution and operation. In this sense, the purpose of Bitcoin mining is what it does. It isn't pre-defined for us to live up to, but rather something "out-there" for us to discover and make use of as best as we can.

You can ask the question, "Where are we heading?" to our emerging space a thousand times. You can ask the whitepaper, the protocol, the developers, operators, and manufacturers. You can ask the whole supply chain and you'll only ever receive a single verifiably true answer—we are headed wherever we will *survive*, and even there we don't know for how long.

This might confuse the common Bitcoiner, who has learned well the dictum to acquire and HODL their coins at all costs. For them, Bitcoin is a passive game, a *via negativa*, where the key requirements are to simply remain patient and not do something dumb—"Stay humble and stack sats," as Matt Odell says. On a long enough timeline, the mechanics of our number-go-up technology perseveres. The Bitcoin miner has no such luxury. We have tied our fate and our wealth to proof-of-work. Our reward comes from innovating and seizing opportunity, not from our infinite modesty and patience. This is the edge we race on, and while the rulebooks are yet to be written, we have learned enough to put a few stakes in the ground and set our proverbial camp around emerging trends.

The first and most banal observation is that Bitcoin mining is fundamentally a business. Not a singular *type* of business, mind you, but a business nonetheless. The only absolute we know in this business of Bitcoin mining is that a Bitcoin miner consumes electricity and receives some reward. We don't know how often it consumes electricity, if or what it pays for that electricity, if it is only rewarded in hash or some additional payment scheme, or if there are any outside stipulations on the consumption of that electricity.

It is worth highlighting the obvious to emphasize our prior point; Bitcoin mining happens "out-there" and not "in-here." Fundamentally, the success of the miner hinges on their ability to operate and maintain a machine in the real world, not on their ability to theorize, test, or convince in the realm of code. The purpose of the system truly is what it does. The machine contributes hashes to the Bitcoin network, but what it does in the world around us stretches far beyond this on a balance sheet of profits and losses.

At the protocol level, Bitcoin miners come and go regularly. In fact, we have a measure for it—the difficulty adjustment. The Bitcoin network pays absolutely no mind to how successful your mining operation is, whether you are mining profitably or at a loss, or how efficiently you are hashing—it only cares whether or not you are contributing and finding valid blocks, and it maintains only one dictum—add blocks to the network at an average of once every 10 minutes. If the blocks come in too fast or too slow, adjust accordingly.

From this initial observation that Bitcoin mining is fundamentally a business, we can extend a second emerging trend—that Bitcoin miners will exist at any and every size, but their profit models will vary widely. Much like Charlie Spears explained above, Bitcoin mining is similar to the oil and gas industry. While entities as large as Exxon and Aramco produce the exact same commodity as a small family office in Oklahoma or a single well operator on personal acreage, all maintain profitable endeavors. The scale of that profit, the resources of the operators, and the particulars of their models change drastically, yet they are simultaneously able to sustain operations in a market. Bob Burnett will continue to scoop up mid-sized sites for distributed operations, while Jason Les will continue to scale massive operations. Both of these models are viable and profitable, and both come with their own risk profiles and benefits.

Looking at businesses of various sizes hardly helps us identify specific trends in Bitcoin mining. However, by looking at the existing world of power and electrical generation, we can begin to peek into the future. Bitcoin miners are tied to their primary input—electricity—so it should be expected that the business models will coincide with sources of generation. In the future, energy producers and electrical generators may fold Bitcoin mining into their operations directly, either as internal departments or with third-party providers. In the same way Erik and the team at Gridless are partnering with generators to plan and execute generation projects, builders in the energy sector may mitigate production risks, demand risks, delays to grid connection, and availability of transmission by bolting on Bitcoin mining operations to their models.

What's even more remarkable is how this style of thinking allows for the immediate monetization of energy projects without governmental or NGO intervention. This establishes a freer market for energy innovation. No longer is a creator at the mercy of a single third party to greenlight or kill their invention. Do you want to use wave action to generate electricity, but don't have approvals to connect to shore power? Try first with onboard Bitcoin mining. Want to prototype a new form of geothermal energy production, but you're limited to an obscure region of Utah? Monetize your proof of concept with a mine in a container.

Bitcoin mining incentivizes generators to build operations for a world of abundance and innovate continuously. At any moment, a generator can use Bitcoin hash price to model profitability based on the highest possible capacity factor, as opposed to modeling expected consumption and assuming growth rates for future demand that may or may not emerge. The Bitcoin network can be thought of as "purchasing" hash rate at every hour of every day, regardless of location or type of generation. This is a truly agnostic marketplace and affords generators the opportunity to maximize every ounce of capacity factor in their operation.

And what is the result of this?

Existing generators stock their operations with mining rigs, ready to flip on when market conditions align. Inventors no longer limp along from pitch to pitch seeking seed funding for a moonshot electrical idea. Instead they partner with a Bitcoin miner or a private financing operation and monetize the business more directly. They do, after all, generate the resource that generates the hardest money on Earth. With a universal buyer—the Bitcoin network—that always prices the market transparently, energy production will grow, and grow, and grow, and the beneficiaries of this tsunami of innovation will be you and me.

How we benefit will not be as obvious as the invention of the Model T. You won't see the roads, stoplights, and gas stations being built and you won't get the wind in your hair. Rather, it will be like most 21st-century inventions, the internet being the best example. It will enable jobs, businesses, and ancillary industries we cannot foresee, and instead of fighting over the domain of legacy industries, it will obsolete them by building an entirely new ocean of opportunities. The originators of the World Wide Web were not incentivized by a future of Snapchat and Instagram models (maybe they would have worked differently if they knew?), but rather the opportunity to fulfill a vision of data sharing across the world. In the same way, Bitcoin miners, driven by their utilitarian and profit-seeking ideologies, enable a world of energy abundance, not knowing what those future sources look like or how they may be obtained.

At this point, you know as well as the author what comes next in the world of Bitcoin mining. There are only four parts to the machine and three physical connections, and with that arrangement of simple pieces we are building a new industry of novel and profitable business entities. You can look into the world yourself and see the abundant thermodynamic slack in our energy procurement, generation, delivery, and consumption systems, and you can envision where Bitcoin mining makes short work of their byproducts.

Waste now has a price.

Heat now has a monetary value.

All energy, regardless of type or location, has a buyer.

Internalizing the significance of this won't send you bouncing from walls or screaming from parapets, but it should embed in you a resounding optimism in a modern world rife with perpetual instability and the impending threat of the unknown. Bitcoin is not simply a system that empowers the user through monetary freedom via the acquisition and custody of an asset. Bitcoin is also a living, breathing network of miners—businesses that enable human flourishing through the pursuit of monetary value and a relationship with energy, the most fundamental of human relationships. It is not for us to determine the course of that path of human flourishing, but rather it is our responsibility to educate and ignite a spark of inquiry—the same spark that has caught so many of us aflame in this young and exciting space.

ENDNOTES

1   "Hashrate and Difficulty," mempool.space, accessed January 4, 2024, https://mempool.space/graphs/mining/hashrate-difficulty#1y.

2   "Ford Model T," Wikipedia, last modified February 16, 2024, https://en.wikipedia.org/wiki/Ford_Model_T#CITEREF FordCrowther1922.

3   "Nikon D50 Overview," *Digital Photography Review*, April 20, 2005, https://www.dpreview.com/products/nikon/slrs/nikon_d50.

4   "Nikon D800 Overview," *Digital Photography Review*, February 7, 2012, https://www.dpreview.com/products/nikon/slrs/nikon_d800.

5   Alec Liu, "Engineering the Bitcoin Gold Rush: An Interview with Yifu Guo, Creator of the First Purpose-Built Miner," *Vice*, March 26, 2013, https://www.vice.com/en/article/aeemzz/engineering-the-bitcoin-gold-rush-an-interview-with-yifu-guo-creator-of-the-first-asic-based-miner.

6   Rebecca Price and Mikelann Scerbo, "Direct Current Power Systems Can Save Energy, So Building Developers Are Getting A New Incentive To Incorporate Them," Alliance to Save Energy, February 26, 2019, https://www.ase.org/blog/direct-current-power-systems-can-save-energy-so-building-developers-are-getting-new-incentive.

7   100 Acres Ranch, last modified January 10, 2023, https://100acresranch.com/.

8   https://support.bitmain.com/hc/en-us/articles/8906244096409-S19-XP-Specifications; https://shop.whatsminer.com/products.

9   "Bitcoin mining control board variations," Braiins.com, last modified September 8, 2023, https://braiins.com/blog/bitcoin-mining-control-board-variations.

10 "Firmware," Wikipedia, last modified January 16, 2024, https://en.wikipedia.org/wiki/Firmware.

11 Whatsminer, last modified January 10, 2023, https://www.whatsminer.com/.

12 "The story behind the ASIC evolution," BLOG.BITMAIN.COM, April 29, 2020, https://blog.bitmain.com/en/tag/antminer-s1/.

13 "S19 XP Specifications," BITMAIN Support, last modified September 8, 2023, https://support.bitmain.com/hc/en-us/articles/8906244096409-S19-XP-Specifications.

14 "What is energy?," U.S. Energy Information Administration, last modified August 16, 2023, https://www.eia.gov/energyexplained/what-is-energy/laws-of-energy.php.

15 Michael Salyor, "Bitcoin is a swarm of cyber hornets," September 18, 2020, https://twitter.com/saylor/status/1307029562321231873?s=20.

16 As of February 2024, 6.25BTC per block.

17 "Block hashing algorithm," Bitcoin Wiki, last modified February 20, 2021, https://en.bitcoin.it/wiki/Block_hashing_algorithm.

18 "Merkle Tree," Wikipedia, last modified February 4, 2024, https://en.wikipedia.org/wiki/Merkle_tree.

19 https://mempool.space/block/000000000000000000014f161e726b342f8b56085accf5205606c56e0ddd3242

20 "Proof of Work," Wikipedia, last modified February 3, 2024, https://en.wikipedia.org/wiki/Proof_of_work; "Proof of Work," Bitcoin Wiki, last modified June 6, 2020, https://en.bitcoin.it/wiki/Proof_of_work.

21 Satoshi Nakamoto, "Bitcoin: A Peer-to-Peer Electronic Cash System," Bitcoin.org, October 31, 2008, https://bitcoin.org/bitcoin.pdf.

22 "Difficulty," Bitcoin Wiki, last modified December 30, 2023, https://en.bitcoin.it/wiki/Difficulty#How_often_does_the_network_difficulty_change.3F.

23 Jake Frankenfield, "Nonce: What It Means and How It's Used in Blockchain," Investopedia, last modified November 22, 2023, https://www.investopedia.com/terms/n/nonce.asp.

24 "Bitcoin Talk," Bitcoin Wiki, last modified March 28, 2023, https://en.bitcoin.it/wiki/BitcoinTalk.

25 "Reasons to mine on Slush Pool," Bitcoin Forum, November 27, 2010, https://bitcointalk.org/index.php?topic=1976.0.

26 "Reasons to mine on Slush Pool," Bitcoin Forum.

27 Foundry, last modified 2024, https://foundrydigital.com/mining-service/foundry-usa-pool/.

28 Luxor, last modified 2024, https://luxor.tech/mining.

29 Braiins, last modified 2024, https://braiins.com/.

30 Lincoin, last modified 2024, https://lincoin.com/.

31 Matjaz Skorjanc, "How mining pools distribute rewards? PPS vs FPPS vs PPLNS," November 11, 2019, https://www.nicehash.com/blog/post/how-mining-pools-distribute-rewards-pps-vs-fpps-vs-pplns#!.

32 "Capacity of the largest solar photovoltaic power plants in the United States as of June 2023," Statistica, last modified June 2023, https://www.statista.com/statistics/1394873/ranking-of-solar-pv-plants-in-the-united-states-by-capacity-2023/.

33 "Electricity Transmission," Institute for Energy Research, n.d., https://www.instituteforenergyresearch.org/electricity-transmission/.

34 "Regional Transmission Organizations/Independent System Operators," Federal Energy Regulatory Commission, last modified January 17, 2024, https://www.ferc.gov/power-sales-and-markets/rtos-and-isos.

35 "Federal Energy Regulatory Commission," Wikipedia, last modified February 2, 2024, https://en.wikipedia.org/wiki/Federal_Energy_Regulatory_Commission.

36 "Electric Power Markets," Federal Energy Regulatory Commission, last modified January 17, 2024, https://www.ferc.gov/electric-power-markets; "Regional Transmission Organization," Wikipedia, last modified April 16, 2021, https://en.wikipedia.org/wiki/Regional_transmission_organization_(North_America).

37 "Regional Transmission Organizations/Independent System Operators," Federal Energy Regulatory Commission.

38 Allison Bailes, "Electricity Demand and the Duck Curve," November 6, 2015, https://www.energyvanguard.com/blog/electricity-demand-and-the-duck-curve/.

39 "Monthly generator capacity factor data now available by fuel and technology," U.S. Energy Information Administration, last modified January 15, 2014, https://www.eia.gov/todayinenergy/detail.php?id=14611

40 Alex Epstein, Fossil Future: Why Global Human Flourishing Requires More Oil, Coal, And Natural Gas–Not Less (New York: Penguin Random House, 2022).

41 Bailes, "Electricity Demand."

42 Katie Surma, "Corruption and Rights Abuses Are Flourishing in Lithium Mining Across Africa, a New Report Finds," Inside Climate News, November 15, 2023, https://insideclimatenews.org/news/15112023/lithium-mining-africa-human-rights-violations-corruption/; "How 'Modern-Day Slavery' Powers The Rechargeable Battery Economy," February 1, 2023, https://www.npr.org/2023/01/31/1152799423/how-modern-day-slavery-powers-the-rechargeable-battery-economy.

43 Lauri Myllyvirta, Aiqun Yu, Flora Champenois, and Xing Zhang, "China permits two new coal power plants per week in 2022," Centre for Research on Energy and Clean Air, February 27, 2023, https://energyandcleanair.org/publication/china-permits-two-new-coal-power-plants-per-week-in-2022/

44 "Total primary energy supply by fuel, 1971 and 2019," International Energy Agency, last modified 2023, https://www.iea.org/data-and-statistics/charts/total-primary-energy-supply-by-fuel-1971-and-2019.

45 "Population Growth," Our World in Data, n.d., https://ourworldindata.org/population-growth.

46 Ann Parker, "Charting the Nation's Energy Use," Lawrence Livermore National Laboratory, February 2021, https://str.llnl.gov/2021-02/simon; "Estimated U.S. Energy Consumption in 2022: 100.3 Quads," Lawrence Livermore National Laboratory, July 2023, https://flowcharts.llnl.gov/sites/flowcharts/files/2023-10/US%20Energy%202022.png.

47 Ken Stewart, "Laws of Thermodynamics," Britannica, last updated January 4, 2024, https://www.britannica.com/science/laws-of-thermodynamics.

48 Nic Carter, Shaun Connell, Brad Jones, Dennis Porter, and Murray A. Rudd, "Leveraging Bitcoin Miners as Flexible Load Resources for Power System Stability and Efficiency," SSRN, November 30, 2023, https://dx.doi.org/10.2139/ssrn.4634256; Joachim Seel, Dev Millstein, Andrew Mills, Mark Bolinger, Ryan Wiser, "Plentiful electricity turns wholesale prices negative," Advances in Applied Energy, November 19, 2021, https://www.sciencedirect.com/science/article/pii/S2666792421000652.

49 "Kansas," U.S. Energy Information Administration, last modified October 2023, https://www.eia.gov/state/?sid=KS.

50 "List of largest hydroelectric power stations," Wikipedia, last modified November 16, 2022, https://en.wikipedia.org/wiki /List_of_largest_hydroelectric_power_stations.

51 "Anexo C," Itaipu Binacional, April 26, 1973, https://www.itaipu .gov.py/sites/default/files/af_df/anexoC_Esp.pdf.

52 Lee Krystek, "Megadam: The Itaipu," October 15, 2011, https:// web.archive.org/web/20140107110217/ http:/www.unmuseum .org/7wonders/megadam.htm; "Itaipu Dam," Wikipedia, last modified February 1, 2024, https://en.wikipedia.org/wiki /Itaipu_Dam.

53 "Paraguay Population 2024," World Population Review, n.d., https://worldpopulationreview.com/countries/paraguay -population

54 Regina Blenda Ayala, "The Itaipu Dam: The Changing Ener-gy Landscape in South America ," Columbia Political Review, September 22, 2023, https://www.cpreview.org/blog/2023/9/ the-itaipu-dam-the-changing-energy-landscape-in-south-america.

55 "Brazil Population 2024," Worldometer, n.d., https://www .worldometers.info/world-population/brazil-population/.

56 Ayala, "The Itaipu Dam."

57 "Golden asteroid: Nasa mission set to launch in 2023," CBBC, November 3, 2022, https://www.bbc.co.uk/news-round/63471074; Ariana Garcia, "NASA to voyage to 'golden asteroid' worth $10,000 quadrillion this fall," June 11, 2023, https://www.chron.com/news/space/article/nasa-golden -asteroid-18144519.php.

58 "Cost of space launches to low Earth orbit," Our World in Data, n.d., https://ourworldindata.org/grapher/cost-space -launches-low-earth-orbit?country=Long+March+4B~Falcon +Heavy~Proton~Saturn+V~Space+Shuttle~Titan+IV~Ariane +5G~Delta+IV+Heavy~Angara~Long+March+5~Scout~Kosmos ~Delta+3000-Series~Delta+3910~Shavit~Pegasus~Start~Rokot ~Taurus~Pegasus+XL~Athena+1~M-V~Shtil~Minotaur+I ~Strela~Falcon+1~Minotaur+IV~Vega~Epsilon~Kuaizhou ~Long+March+11~Electron~Shian+Quxian.

59 "Prospecting for Oil and Natural Gas," Stanford Energy, October 2, 2023, https://understand-energy.stanford.edu/energy -resources/fossil-fuel-energy/prospecting-oil-and-natural-gas.

60 "Drilling, Completing, and Producing from Oil and Natural Gas Wells," Stanford Energy, October 2, 2023, https://understand -energy.stanford.edu/energy-resources/fossil-fuel-energy /drilling-completing-and-producing-oil-and-natural-gas-wells.

61 "Prospecting for Oil and Natural Gas," Stanford Energy.

62 "Understanding methane emissions," International Energy Agency, last modified 2023, https://www.iea.org/reports/global -methane-tracker-2023/understanding-methane-emissions #abstract

63 "Understanding methane emissions," International Energy Agency.

64 https://netl.doe.gov/sites/default/files/2020-12/Stranded -Natural-Gas-Roadmap-04142020.pdf

65 https://electronics.stackexchange.com/questions/668843/how -much-of-the-power-drawn-by-a-chip-turns-into-heat

66 https://www.thermopedia.com/content/841/

67 https://www.thermopedia.com/content/841/

68 Timothy Thiele, "How to Determine Your Electrical Service Amps," last modified November 15, 2022, https://www .thespruce.com/electrical-service-size-of-my-home-1152752.

69 Anthony Capkun, "An Introduction to K-Rated Transformers," February 5, 2011, https://www.ebmag.com/an-introduction -to-k-rated-transformers-9944/.

70 "Bitcoin Hashrate Index," Hashrate Index, last modified February 23, 2024, https://data.hashrateindex.com/chart/bit coin-hashprice-index.

71 "The purpose of a system is what it does," Wikipedia, last modified February 12, 2024, https://en.wikipedia.org/wiki/The _purpose_of_a_system_is_what_it_does.

ACKNOWLEDGMENTS

First, to my incredible wife Elsa, the gravitational constant that holds our little family together. Your unending love and care has made me a better husband, father, and human being, and has undoubtedly seeped into the pages of this book. Your patience, near endless, was only truly challenged by the addition of two Bitmain S9s to the guest bathroom of our 1,000 square foot fifth-story apartment.

To Joe Rodgers and Neil (RoninMiner), for deciding it was a fabulous idea to buy a pallet of S9s from the team at Kaboomracks for the sole purpose of testing, preparing, and selling them to other curious Bitcoiners. Your shared traits of endless curiosity and drive has been an inspiration to my own learning and building in Bitcoin. While Elsa might disagree, I thank you for sending me those first two machines.

To the terminally online community of Bitcoin Twitter, or X or whatever we're supposed to call it nowadays. You are the strangest family reunion I have ever been to, yet I wouldn't be satisfied anywhere else. In no other space can one befriend hobbyists, builders, corporate executives, regenerative ranchers, core developers, or anonymous laser eyed cyber hornets, and get anything done with any degree of proficiency. Somehow it works. Your incisive ideas and feedback have enriched and challenged me in ways I never expected, and I'm thankful for all of you. (Well most of you, but I'll put up with the rest.)

To all of the bright minds at Bitcoin Magazine Publishing, particularly publisher Ellen Sullivan. You have been an absolute pleasure to work with. Your feedback has been sage, and your ability to keep this project moving forwards is unparalleled.

To editor Olson Pook, who with a keen eye and a few flicks of the keyboard worked absolute magic into the organization and coherence of this text.

Finally, to you, the curious reader. I'm so glad you've taken the time to explore this fascinating world of Bitcoin Mining. I hope you've got the bug in the same way I do—that pressing urge to understand this infantile ecosystem and make sense of the apparently disparate parts. It's trite to say, but we are truly so early, and there is much work to be done. I hope this book can inspire you to find your own way to contribute to that work.

ABOUT THE AUTHOR

Robert Warren is an experienced entrepreneur with a history in growth and operations. His technical background in Philosophy and Psychological research, combined with a masters in Education, uniquely positions him in the Bitcoin community to better help explain this technology and its cultural implications. He currently works with Riot Platforms as the Manager of Mining Projects and Operations Analysis.

www.ingramcontent.com/pod-product-compliance
Lightning Source LLC
Chambersburg PA
CBHW031852200326
41597CB00012B/378